CUSTOMERS LIKE YOU MAKE ME WANT TO GO BACK TO BEING A HOOKER

In Memory of Buffalo Jim

PAT NOLAND

authorHOUSE®

AuthorHouse™
1663 Liberty Drive
Bloomington, IN 47403
www.authorhouse.com
Phone: 1-800-839-8640

First published by AuthorHouse 8/14/2009

ISBN: 978-1-4389-8183-3 (sc)

Printed in the United States of America
Bloomington, Indiana

This book is printed on acid-free paper.

In Memory of Buffalo Jim

A. TABLE OF CONTENTS

B: DEDICATIONS

I have a lot of p.eople that I have to thank for this impossible endeavor.

TO: My son, Michael, who is my life, gave me encouragement and money.

TO: Gloria, who inspired me to write this book.

TO: Sylvia who gave me home and hearth.

TO: My Grandchildren, Michael, Michael, and Cheyenne.

TO: Buffalo Jim, whose hatchet was always flying to the bad guys. I might add, that Jim gave up his life for standing up to the Mafia.

TO: Belfast Computers, who helped me through my broken down computer. At one point, I was just out of money and Ryan fixed my computer for a post-dated check. I asked Ryan, one time what he had done with one of my checks. He told me that me "I have made an airplane out of your check."

TO: To Carolyn, who helped my grandchildren beyond the call of duty.

To: Buddy Dow: My editor who is witty,patient, and my friend. I am writing a piece about him as the most unforgettable character I have known for the Reader's Digest.

(Does anyone every read this magazine?)

C: CAST OF CHARACTERS

Doormen at the Bellagio's Hotel: Steve, Ron, Buddy,Lee, and Thomas.

Doormen at the MGM Hotel: Carlos, Brian,Patrick, and Joe.

Doormen at the Venetian Hotel: Fino, Scott, Vennie, Brian, and all of the new doormen.

Doormen at the Mandalay Bay Hotel: Rick, Frank, Joey,and Scott.

Bill Shranko:	Manager of Yellow, Checker, and Star Taxicab Companies
Jay Nady:	Owner of A-Cab Company.
Charlie Frias:	Owner of Union, Ace, Vegas, North Las Vegas Taxicab, and a Limousine services. That right folks, five different infinities.
Pete Eliades:	Part owner of Yellow. Star, and Checker Cab.
Taxicab Authority:	Policies all taxicabs in Las Vegas.
John Plunket:	Ex-President of Taxicab Authority.
Natalie Infermo:	Works for the Taxicab Authority.
Steve Miller:	Writer for the Las Vegas Tribune.
Buffalo Jim:	The best guy in the world.
Rick Rizzolo:	Owner of the Crazy Horse Too.
John Sannon:	"Hound Dawg." Owner of the web site www.vegascabbie.com

Talley:	Owner of web site vegascabbie.net.
Ruthie Jones:	Nice President of the union.
Chris Harris:	Managing Editor of Trip Magazine.
Dan Shepard:	Writer for the Taxi, Limo Magazine
Jeff German:	Reporter for the Las Vegas Sun Newspaper
George Knapp:	Editor for the Las Vegas Mercury Newspaper
Oscar Goodman:	Famous Ex-Mayor of Las Vegas

ADVOCATES FOR THE TAXICAB DRIVERS:

Hound Dawg:	Worked for Frias: Fired
Daryl Poleman	Worked for Yellow Cab: Fired
Dave Sanders:	Worked for Union, and A-Cab: fired.
Steve La Croix:	Fired from A-Cab.
Ray Stultz:	A-Cab, Whittlesea,and Union Cab: Fired
Jim Talley:	Worked for Union Cab: fired.
Patty:	Jim being fired after fifteen years is the one that I am most out raged about.

Writers for www.cabbievegas.com Gypsy, Antenna Ball, Elliot Ness, Vegas Book, and Okey.

Writers for vegascabbie.net Jim Talley, Radio Rules 2 Shocked, The cab Files, Patty Noland, Pro-cabbie, Mega Dave, Las Vegas Republican.

D: EXPRESSIONS OF THE TAXICAB BUSINESS

Go Through lane:	You only have one lane that moves forward all of the time. You cannot drop off passengers in this lane.
Staging:	This is where the taxicabs wait to pick up passengers.
Wide and Waiting:	Too many cabs are waiting for fares.
Fares:	Customers in your cab.
Moving up the line:	The cabs are moving up to pick up.
Move up, Move up, Move up:	We have to move up our cabs fast.
Lining up at the hotels:	We are behind cabs that are waiting for rides at the hotel.
Coming up the line:	We are moving our car up behind the the other cabs.
Lining up right:	When you go into a hotel, you drop your fare off in the right place. This also goes for picking up people. (I never line up right. and the doormen are always screaming at me, but, not too loud.)
Extras:	People who wait at the cab company hoping that someone will not show up so they can drive that day.

Trip Charge:	The amount of money that the cab companies take out for every trip that the driver's make everyday.
Taxicab Driver's Book:	The sheet of papers,which shows your boss and the taxicab authority, how many hours you are working, and how much money you bring in.
D.I.	Desert Inn Road or the former Desert Inn Hotel. Mr. Steve Wynn owns the D.I,and he has now called his new hotel,"La Reeve."
Higher Book:	Drivers who make the most money for the taxicab companies
Rolling the meter:	The cab driver keeps the meter running so he doesn't have to pay the trip charge on the next ride.
Taxicab Authority Card:	This is a plastic picture with your name, and your taxicab number.
Front Loading:	If a customer tries to take a cab out of line, waiting for their own pick up.
VC	Abbreviation of web site of www.vegascabbie.com

E: THANK YOU

Thank You	Bellagio's Hotel. To all of the doormen at Bellagio;s, Steve, Buddy, Lee, and Thomas
MGM Hotel:	Carlos, Bryan,Patrick, and Joe.
Venetian Hotel:	Steve, Scott, Fino,
Mandalay Bay:	Frank, Rick, Joey, and Lauren
Paris Hotel:	Scott, and Charles
Mirage Hotel:	Frank
Hilton Hotel:	Michael and gruff doorman at the Hilton Hotel.
Luxor Hotel:	Dale.
To all of the airport police:	Linda, Scott, Rick.
To the good guys:	Mark, Paul, George, Pablo Cruz, Helen and her husband. To the great gals in the office of Yellow Cab Company,and Frias, starting with Rita.
To the taxicab Authority:	Scott, Mr Martinez, and to all of the girls in the office at the Taxicab Authority.
Best company to work for:	Lucky cab.
Best Supervisor:	Bob Hopkins.
Best Manager:	Bill Sharnko.

F: AS LBJ SAID TO ALL OF HIS COUNTRY MEN

I have tried to keep the flavor of the letters that were written into the sites. For the rest of the book, I have done the editing myself and my spelling and grammar leaves something to be desired. In Chapter 15, I have written an article about my spelling and punctuation. All, I can say to the doorman, Carlos, who teaches a class about Shakespeare. I tried.

CHAPTER ONE
TIPPING IN LAS VEGAS

Patty: First of all, Dear Readers: I will give you my guide on how to tip people. I feel that everyone should tip the taxicab drier, doorman and the maid five dollars per service. Also, you should reach under your bed, where you keep you keep your serious money, and give the bartender three to five dollars every round. You should also tip the services, waitresses, or waiters three to five dollars per every ten dollars of the cost of your dinner, lunch, breakfast, tea time, and buffet time.

This article was written by Frank Lucero for the Trip Sheet magazine in Las Vegas.

TIPPING

TAXICAB DRIVER: One who drives you all over the checker board.

TAXICAB GUIDELINE FOR PASSENGERS

Under no circumstances ever touch, pet, or grope a female cab driver. Never proposition them. (That is really in bad taste, (no matter how horny you are.) Exceptions; A friendly handshake or a pat on the back is okay.

Patty: Of course, if it is Robert DeNero, play on.

SEX IN A CAB;

No sex is allowed in the cab. Some people believe what they see on television and have become uninhibited while visiting Sin City. If you want to have sex while in the cab, offer the driver a big fat tip up front. Fifty dollars ought to cover it. A rubber is extra. I once sold a condon for twenty dollars.

LOADING LUGGAGE;

Your cabby just loaded your over sized packed suitcases, it is not his fault you do not know how to pack for a trip. A good tip is three to five dollars for three packs of luggage. Anything over three is on you.

BIG TIPPERS:

To receive the high roller treatment when taking a cab or, if you desire that great service, flash the money. Nothing makes the cabby happier or more professional than a big tip,

Around ten dollars, although if you really want all the extras: doors opened, tips to the hottest clubs, where to pick up chicks, or where the all-male revues are, best massages, and use of a cell phones, a large tip of twenty bucks is suggested.

Patty: I might add, up front with the tip.

Frank: LOCATION IS EVERYTHING;

Whether you are staying at the Belalgio's, Venetian, Monte Carlo,or Golden Nugget, one thing is certain, you have good taste and maybe a few dollars. Drivers know this so expect good service. A larger tip is also expected, so don't get cheap now and hide behind, I'm frugal," and maintain my integrity by not spreading my wealth around, "Vegas is not a place for tight wad flints."

NO CHANGE

Never hand a cabbie coins and do not expect coins back. Always round your fare upward. Example: Nine dollars and ten cents becomes ten dollars, plus tip, four dollars upward, and ninety cents become five dollars, plus tip.

ALWAYS REMEMBER TO TIP THE CABBY

Never ask the cabby for change from a fifty or a one hundred-dollar bill. Get your money exchanged at the casino before taking a cab or else be prepared to pay for the taxicab driver's time while you scurry, and scramble to find change. Many passengers knowingly do this at the airport, and expect a free ride,especially on those small trips from the MGM or The Hard Rock. SO, DON'T TRY IT! You wouldn't consider letting him have the whole five or one-hundred dollars because you have not change your money, and don't stand, there looking stupid, or disappointed when he doesn't give you your freebie.

ASK THE DOORMAN FOR THE CHANGE.

Patty: I have always been to shy to tell a customer that he will be paying for the time that it takes takes him to get his change. If you do not have enough money to get to the airport, go to the MGM and ask for John, he will usually ask you if you have a checking account and have you write a check. Please be sure to give him a generous tip. John has told me that he has never been beaten.

Frank: SMOKES

Always ask permission before lighting up cigarette in a taxi. If you insist on smoking in a cab, tip the driver. Drivers hate the smoke and the risk of cancer and other things like lung disease but will tolerate the smoke for a few bucks. Cigar smokers should know to roll down the window while puffing one stogy. If you're smoking a fine cigar. Make sure you offer one to the cabby.

Patty: Cigarette smoke absolutely makes me ill.

POT SMOKING

Sorry,   Dudes,Homier,and   brothers,but,you   cannot   smoke Marijuana in a Las Vegas Taxicab. Smoke your herb before the cab ride, or ask the driver to pull the cab over while you smoke it up, but remember the meter will continue to run while you are re-catching "a buzz." Also a larger than normal tip is recommended. No pinch of the chronic stash for late tips is allowed.

Patty: Thank God, I do not have that problem. All pot has ever done for me is to make me hungry.

CASH DEPOSTS

If your ride is expected to be more than fifteen dollars, a cash deposit of twenty dollars is preferred. If you live in a high-risk neighborhood such as North Town, East Bonanza area or any of the letter street named D, J, or H, you should always volunteer cash depots. Don't be offended when the cab driver demands the money.

COFFEE AND DONUTS

There is nothing more annoying than early morning tourists with their Cappuccino's Java Expresser, and cups of coffee,

If you insist on drinking coffee in the cab, bring your driver's a donut or bagel, or face the possibility of a bumpy ride.

TURN OFF THE METER

Never ask the cabby to turn off the meter, never try to bribe the cabby with lines such as, "I'll give you a big tip, and I'll make it worth your while." Cabbies see right through these lies and have found these types or fares are only worth a few bucks. Besides it is illegal to drive with the meter off! (Yean right.) Don't get upset and angry because your driver refuses to turn the meter off. After all, you are in Vegas and headed to a casino where you are probably going to lose your money gambling. or spend it on some really nice souvenirs like T-shirts that read "I lost my ass in Vegas." So, don't ask!

Well, I hope you know that was only fun and not a real guideline, or was it?

Patty: I do not go anywhere unless I can tip, and tip big.

CHAPTER TWO
HOW I BECAME A TAXICAB DRIVER

So, there I was living in San Francisco, working on computers; I had arthritis so bad that I was living on Vicodin. I had to tell my boss, who was to the right of "Louie the 14th" "I know that I was at Paradigm Health Care last year, but I do not remember Thanksgiving or Xmas.

What do I do? I moved to Las Vegas and become a taxicab driver. I have always thought that the "grass was greener on the other side of the fence." Well, it is not, but on occasions, I have made the right move. It was so expensive in San Francisco that I was continually looking for new place to live. One of my co-workers said to me, "Why not Las Vegas?" I am the eternal escapist; I started looking at the out-of-town newspapers.

There were tons of jobs listed in the Las Vegas newspapers. When my arthritis started getting worse, I thought to myself, "I am not living in San Francisco, I am living in beautiful downtown Antioch. It's time to move on."

I made the decision to look into the job situation in Nevada. I flew to Las Vegas and started looking for jobs at the casinos. I had been a bank proof operator at three different banks in San Francisco, so I though I could work with money and be a cage cashier. At the casinos, they usually start you out as a cashier, if you do not have any experience with the hotel business.

I was at Caesar's Palace Hotel, and I had the feeling that my interview was not going well. Because, I was 63 years old, Caesar's was not going to hire me. All of the hotels give great benefits, and they do not want a employee who is in bad health using their benefits up front.

Most cashiers start at around nine dollars an hour. Families move to Las Vegas, and they all work at one, or more hotels. The first thing that they do is to buy a home, and then all pull together.

I was on the depressed side, I was telling all my troubles to a taxicab driver, and the cab driver said to me,"Why don't you become a taxicab driver?" It sounds like fun, doesn't it? Driving around talking to the,"Powers to Be."

Patty: My backing up leaves something to be desired.

Driver: You are not suppose to back up,you are just suppose to go forward. Go, and talk to Bill Shranko, the general manager at Yellow Cab.

I had a great resume, so I went to see Bill at Yellow Cab. He looked at my recommendations and he said, "I want someone of your caliber working for me."

Patty: I could not believe it. I had a job. I have a speech problem and it is not so easy for me to find work. I told all my friends, and they cracked up about me being a taxicab drivers. I didn't care, I was on my way!

Patty: Will my speech be an impediment?

Bill: At least you speak English. I just want you to go out there and have fun.

Patty: Hah! Little did I know that all Las Vegas taxicab companies lose about sixty percent of their drivers every month. I did not fully understand that all cab drivers work twelve hours a day. I had visions of meeting my next ex-husband, but after working twelve hours a day, I could not go out with Richard Burton, if he was out there, and he is not there.

In California, I had a driver's license that stated that my age was fifty-eight years old, although I was sixty-three. Taking off five years seemed like a good idea to me, at the time, because I thought it would be easier to get a job. I had to go down to the Nevada Department of Motor Vehicles to change my age on my license because the FBI checks all of the taxicab driver's license applicants closely for criminal background. It is too bad that the Department of Motor Vehicles does not check the strip club owner's background, and while we are at it, the taxicab owner's past.

I would probably not come to Las Vegas, If I had known that I was going to have to give up those years.

This is my resume:

October 14, 1999
To whom it may concern.

Every successful company strives to bring its employees to optimum productivity through training, focus, and encouragement. Sometimes a company is privileged to have a special person, who right from the beginning sets the standard to which all others are compared. At Paradigm Health Care Services, that person is Patty Noland.

Rarely, have I seen anyone in this company, or elsewhere with Patty's sense of devotion to the task at hand. Even, more unusual is the person who year in and year out performs at such impressive levels.

Data entry can be fiercely dull work, yet accuracy is critical especially in our business. By our measure which is careful and specific, Patty completely eclipses any of the other kier on the staff, and her accuracy is reliable with in parameters. Just as importantly, she takes particular care with difficult input documents and may be trusted to bring questionable items to her supervisor's attention.

Patty: I drove Paul crazy with my questions, but I also knew how to make my score higher then it should be. I knew that I was going to be a great taxicab driver.

Paul: I offer my enthusiastic recommendation of Ms. Noland capabilities to any company fortunate enough to merit her consideration.

Sincerely,
Paul, the good guy
Operations Manager.

Patty: This is what I was really doing.

April 1998 to June 1998.	Mercenary in Serb Army. I took part in wiping out villages. I am sorry about all of the people I killed.
March 1995 to April 1997.	Secretary to the Nazi Party. I tried to have Steven Spielberg assassinated.
Jan1994 to February 1994.	Did thirty days in jail for pandering
December 1992 to February 1943	Took over Sally Stanford's Bordello. I was really happy to meet all of the nice men whose wives did not understand them.
November 1990 to December 1990.	Did a month in jail for drug dealing.
June 1990 to November 1990.	Sold drugs in San Francisco. It did not really count, as they were just pharmaceutical drugs.

Patty Noland

CHAPTER THREE
FIRST EXPERIENCES OF BEING A TAXICAB DRIVER IN LAS VEGAS

From here on out, I will refer to Yellow, Checker, and Star taxicab companies as YCS, if I feel like it.

On my first day as a cab driver, I was absolutely terrified. I had never driven a cab before. In fact, I am a terrible driver. I hate cars; they remind me of men, because they are always breaking down.

Bob, my supervisor put me in a van. I was so frightened that I do not even remember driving. Some of the mistakes that I made were comical. I had customers who wanted to go to the Rio Hotel, I was behind the hotel, in front of the hotel, on the side of the hotel, and I just could not get to that damn hotel.

The Rio looked so close that I felt like I could touch it. Finally, my customers got out of my car and told me, "they would walk to the Rio."

The next three days, Bob put me in a sedan. I had passengers showing me the way to the Convention Center, and to the MGM Hotel. One customer told me that "I should take some time, look around and get my bearings." On my 4th day, I was in a van again, I told Bob, "I was going home and returning to San Francisco."

I knew that I was in a trap, and I had to go back to work as a taxicab driver. I neither had the money for my lease, or to move back to San Francisco.

I went back down to YCS, and talked to Bill, and told him, "I wanted to try to be a taxicab driver. Please do not put me in a van." Bill was so nice to me, anyone else would have been fired. I would be sorry later on about driving a car with three hundred-fifty thousand miles on it. I was so naive about driving a cab that I use to run around my car to adjust my rear view mirrors. Finally someone took pity on me, and told me that you can adjust the mirrors from the inside of the car.

Dear Readers: Do you remember when gas attendants would put in the gas, water, and oil in your car? Once a week, I would have to drive a "test cab," to find out how the car performed. I would pay the gas attendant two dollar to put the gas in, change the water, and check the oil.

When you move to Las Vegas, if you have a job, all you have to do is pay the first month rent, otherwise you have to pay the first and lasts months rent. I faxed Bill and, "asked him to send me a letter stating that I was going to be working for YCS." He faxed me back immediately giving me the necessary letter. I wrote to Bill telling him that I was going to "name my first born after him."

My first ride was to Bellagio's Hotel, only because I could figure out that we were suppose to go through their tunnel to pick up their rides. Steve Wynn, the former owner of Bellagio's put in a tunnel because he considered taxicabs to be eyes sores. I do not know if Mr. Wynn meant the taxicabs or the drivers.

Two old ladies came out to me cab, and asked me to take them to the Imperial Palace Hotel. I looked at Ron, the doorman and asked him, "Where is the Imperial Palace?"

Ron: You do not know where the Imperial Palace is?"

Patty: It is right down the street. I had just taken the taxicab test, and I had forgotten everything. The two little old ladies said to me,"We are not riding with you,"and removed themselves from my cab."

Spectacular beginning, don't you think?

A few days later, I was at the Venetian, I picked up a couple that wanted to go to the Gun Store. On the way over, I told Bonnie and Clyde that I wished that "America was like England, and Japan, and would get rid of guns." They were both from Chicago and it is very difficult to get a legal gun. (I never knew that Chicago was so progressive.)

When we arrived at the gun store, I saw a a big sign that read, "If you do not vote for Bush, don't be surprised when Gore's deputies come and take your guns away." I was cracking up, while my lady customer was in an enclosed area, shooting a machine gun. She was probably trying to think of some way to smuggle the gun out of Las Vegas.

Patty: I was sitting in my cab waiting for my customers; my fare was up to thirty dollars, and I started to think that this might be a pretty good tip for me. On the way back to the Venetian, I completely prostituted myself. I told my customers that if they wanted guns, it is their constitutional right to have guns. They should have an AK-47, or a machine gun. She could have taken part in the Bank of American massacre a few years ago in California. I then told Bonnie and Clyde that I was going to join the NRA. (UGH)

I do not understand this fascination with guns. I could not kill a deer or any other animal. If I was the one who had to kill the cow, I would become a vegetarian.

What surprised me is how expensive guns are? I wondered how people can afford to buy these guns. Of course, if you are a thief that is robbing everyone, you can take the money off of your income tax.

One customer compared guns to cars. He told me, "guns do not run over people." Another, fare said, "What do you want to do, use a knife? You will get blood all over the place."

Patty: I do not want to kill anyone except my ex-husband, and if I arranged to have him killed, I would probably be sat up with a under cover cop. like the poor woman In Seattle.

I was at Bellagio's one morning at 7:30 A.M. Two black guys jumped into my car, and asked me take them to the MGM Hotel. I looked at the lead taxicab driver on the line, and he told me to take the fare. He was much more experienced then me, so he probably knew that they were loaded.

In my car, they started throwing things and being verbally abusive. I jumped the red light turning into the MGM, hoping that a police officer would be there. Naturally, the police were not in the area. I was doing thirty-five miles an hour over speed bumps. When we arrived at the door, I got some money out of my drunken customers, jumped out of my cab and took my keys, and ran to John to tell him what had happened. Both customers in my car got out and started being verbally abusive to all of the people coming out of the MGM.

It seems that one of these fellows had lost his hat; you should have seen this guy running around asking all of the taxicab drivers if they had his hat?

When he realized that no one had his hat, he was absolutely irate. He tried to hit the girl on the door. John, then stepped in and was hit. I realized that my customers had given me a one hundred dollar bill. John told me to get in my car and keep the hundred dollars, because I deserved it, and to leave. I probably would have kept the money one way or another.

I was out at the airport, and I got a call on my car radio telling me to go back to the MGM. I thought that the customers wanted their money back, but when I returned to the MGM, the manager just wanted a report about what had happened. I asked the manager how he knew that I was driving the cab. He pointed to the cameras on the door; I was on camera, the manager told me that they had seen me running up to the door of the MGM. In Las Vegas, they have everyone on camera. I just hope that the camera is not on in your bedroom.

I asked the manager, if the customers had enough money to go home."

Manager: They are going to have to change their travel plans because they are going to jail.

Patty: I have always been a big time liberal, not wanting anyone to go to jail. This was the first time that I had been involved with people that did not know me, and wanted to hurt me. I was so happy that these guys were going to be locked up. I would have loved being there when they came out of their stupor, and realized that they were in the Las Vegas jail. The Vegas police do not take kindly to people that are drunk and destroying the door of a hotel. It ended up that one of the rap customers had a record with warrants against him, he had to come back to Las Vegas and do some time.

I use to like to go to the strip clubs in the morning, but after a few instances, I passed.

I went to the Barbary coast one morning, and the paramedics were just leaving. The doorman brought a girl out, and put her in my car. She was so loaded on drugs, and alcohol that she could not tell me where she lived. I looked in her wallet, and she told me that she had just moved a few days ago. The door told me, "Just take her anywhere, and drop her off." I asked the door "wonder if she is raped or killed, I am not just throwing this girl away."

I asked the door to call security in the hotel. You will not believe this next one, security at the Barbary Coast told the door that "she was now the cab driver's problem." I nearly flipped out. I said to the door, "she has been getting loaded and drunk in your hotel and she is my problem?" "Yes." I noticed a police car in the parking lot. I asked the door to "call the police." The door told me, "the policeman was downstairs shaving."

She started throwing up, and I lost all of my compassion for her. I physically removed her from my car, and I ran around and locked my door. I rolled up my window and I said to the door, "Now she is your problem."

One, morning, I was over at Crazy Horse Too and this kid in a wheel chair got into my cab. He told me that he had spent all of his money on a stripper, and she was sending him back to the Rio Hotel to get some more money. I tired to talk him out of going back to the Horse. I told him "to go to the Chicken Ranch, where prostitutions legal. He was not going to get anything sexually from the stripper." He said to me, "She is such a great talker." I yelled at him, "What do you expect? These girls were born talking and fucking."

When we arrived at the Rio, "he asked me to wait for him," which would have been a good ride for me. I told him, "No," because ripping off a person in a wheel chair is beyond the pale for me. I talked to someone who worked at the Crazy Horse and she told me that a lots of men come into the club and will give the girl's five thousand dollars just to talk to them.

I had a gentlemen that was part of the Cigarette convention. This customer was probably trying to figure out how he could put more nicotine in the cigarettes that he was selling. My fare told me that he did not feel guilty about all of the people, who became ill or ended up having cancer.

I had two Germans in my car, and I asked my customers, what they disliked about Americans?"

Rudolf: You do not eat all of the food on your plate. You use too much air conditioning.

Patty: How much money do you make?

Rudolph: I make about about two thousand dollars a month."

Patty: How much money do you pay in taxes?

Rudolf: About eight hundred dollars a month.

Patty: I laughed and told him, "You cannot afford air condition.

Rudolf: You are right.

Patty: But, the part that kills me is when the foreigners tell me that Americans are too arrogant. We are so sure of our importance, we are overbearing, and haughty. In other wards, we think that we are better then anyone else.

I really do not feel this way. If someone starves to death in India, I do not value my life more then his or her life. I am just happy that I live in a country where I do not have to eat all of my food on my plate. I am really getting tired of hearing the United States being called, "The Great Satan," particularly when we honestly try to help these third world countries.

I had two gentlemen in my car from Iraq. They told me that "Americans are Grandfather's to the world." I replied to my customers, "Oh come off it, and really tell me how you feel?"

Iraqis: Americans are very naive.

Patty: In other wards, we are fools. These Iraqi's had citizenship in America.

At the airport, the gardener was watering the plants, all of the water had seeped down on the freeway. At least six taxicabs were in a collision. A limousine had completely turned over. All of the cab drivers were probably cited for this fraction of the law. Can't you just see the drivers going up to the airport at night time, dumping water on the plants? Later on, I will give you, Dear Readers, all of the gossip at the airport.

Scott, who has worked at the airport for twenty years, was upset. He was down in the pit, screaming at the drivers to move up the line.

Patty: What is wrong?

Scott: I am tired of being a babysitter for the drivers to move up the line. I am going to "86th" the cabs drivers who do not move faster.

Patty: The airport has a loud buzzer that will ring to let the taxicab drivers know that they had better get moving to pick up their customers.

Three guys were in my car, and they told me that they had been to the Red Rooster Night Club.

Patty: I have never heard of the place.

Lotharios: It is a night club where you can go with your "woman of the night," change partners, and fuck someone else right in front of everyone."

Patty: I could not believe this, but when I went back to the taxi yard, other drivers told me this was true. Quite of few of the clubs offer this service. (ask you taxicab driver) I know that in other cities, exchanging partners goes on, but in Las Vegas, anything goes.

I had a Chinese man in my car, I asked him, "if the Chinese really believe that we purposely bombed their Embassy in Belgrade, Yugoslavia. Why would the United States do something like that? We do billions of dollars of business with China? He replied "Just the illiterate Chinese."

I had a another customer in my car that often went to Colombia. I asked him "if all of the money we send to Colombia was really helping the Colombians fight the drug trade." My customer replied, "the government builds malls with the money."

Patty: I bet that Columbia is really grateful to us.

I had a customer in my car that was from India. I asked him, "about the money that the United States sends to India." He told me "India was upset because we try to tell them what to do with the money."

Patty: There is one way to stop all of these problems, just do not take our money any more.

I picked up a girl, who wanted to drive a cab. I told her that it is hard work, and if she could do anything else, she should try and find a different occupation.

Potential taxi cab driver: I do not have any training to do anything else.

Patty: Get a job driving a cab in Oklahoma, if you like it, then move to the big city. I then advised her, "do not drive in Las Vegas."

On March 14, 2002, a day that will live infamy, I picked up Ray and his family. They were from New York City, and they were going to the Mandalay Hotel. My customer was young, about nineteen. On the way over to the hotel, Ray started throwing up.

I stated yelling. "You are throwing up in my car, which was pretty obvious." He was really throwing up, not gagging, or spitting but throwing up. I said to Ray, "Why didn't you tell me that you were sick, so I could have pulled my cab over?" Ray kept telling me, "he was sorry."

I asked his Mother if he had been drinking. Like all good mothers, she said, "he has not been partaking of the bubbly." The Father (or husband) was very nonchalant about the whole thing. I radioed in to Friars cab Company and told them. "my fare was sick and that I was returning my customers to the MGM."

When we arrived, he asked his Mother, "If she would walk in front of him,"because he was so embarrassed, he did not want anyone to see that he had become ill.

Patty; I felt sorry for him at this point. She gave me an extra fifteen dollars.

When I returned to the yard, the next driver nearly died, I do not blame him. The night driver asked me, "if it was really my last drive which is ridiculous?" How could I pick up anyone else with my car in that condition? We each gave the kid in the body shop five dollars to clean up the car. The night driver told me, "I should have asked for fifty dollars or at least twenty-five dollars, because I had to pay someone to clean up the car."

Patty: This was my first ride where someone was sick in my car. Let's hope that it was the last time. Once I had a Limo driver from Los Angeles and he told me that he charges his customers one hundred dollars for getting sick in his car. I told the parents of the boy that I was going to put this incident in my book, and they promised me they would buy the book.

People who have arthritis often exchange notes with me. One customer told me, "I have to take care of my Mother, who is close to ninety years old. She is in a wheel chair, and cannot bathe or go to the bathroom by herself. She also has to wear a diaper."

Patty; We both agreed that it is essential to put in your will that you do not want to be kept alive beyond a certain point. There was a slight bitterness in his voice about being tied down to an ailing parent.

I gave my son a living will. He told me that if he had to make a decision, and was standing with an attorney telling him that there was a hundred thousand dollars in royalties in the bank, Michael would say, "I want my Mommy."

I had a bad day, and a customer got into my car. He told me that I did not know what a bad day was like. On a different occasion, Thomas arrived in Las Vegas, and immediately went rafting. It took Thomas thirty minutes going down the river, and three, and a half hours getting back up to the top of the river.

He then went into the Las Vegas Hilton to gamble, and he lost seven hundred, and fifty dollars. He could not believe it. He went back to the tables and lost another eight hundred dollars.

Thomas had complimentary tickets to Sheffield and Roy Show, and he thought the show started at eight thirty P.M. The only problem was that the show started at eight o'clock. He and his friend had to stand in the back of the theater, you must understand that these tickets to Sheffield and Roy cost about one hundred dollars a piece.

Since one of the trainers was almost mauled to death, I do think that the hotel features this animal act any more. Thomas came back to the hotel and lost some more money. My friend, was staying at the Las Vegas Hilton on the top floor. Thomas was sitting on his bed, hating the world when the building started to shake. Las Vegas was having an earthquake. He ran down the stairs out into the street. So, you can see, a bad day can get worse. What amazed me is that Thomas came back to Las Vegas at all.

A black guy in my car told me that O.J. Simpson was innocent. He said, "Where did all of the blood go?" I replied to him, "you sure have given me a lot to think about O. J. innocences."

Isn't O.J, the dumbest person in the world?

If I killed someone, and got a way with it, I would have walked the whitest, narrowest road for the rest of my life. He created a facade of being a good guy, but he was just a jerk.

Las Vegas is upset about the Unite States wanting to leave their nuclear waste in the Yucca Mountains, which is only one hundred miles from North Las Vegas. I had an environmentalist is my car, and she told me that we should be worrying about the people who work in the cleaners with all of the fumes.

One woman I picked up was so mad at the slot machines on the strip that she was going downtown, never to return. She told me, "the slot machines on the strip do not pay off."

Patty: I understand the best hotels in Las Vegas that pay off are the Horseshoe, and the Four Queens which are both downtown. Most of these hotels play Black Jack with one deck, while the hotels on the strip play with three or four decks. If they catch you counting, they make you leave. I feel that this is very unfair. If you are smart enough to win, you should be able to win. But, I am not in charge of the gaming commission, because if I was, that would be the first rule that I would change.

I picked up two gentlemen gamblers from the Venetian one morning, and they told me, "We have lost all of our money."

Patty: What kind of work do you do?

Gamblers: We are stock brokers from St. Louis.

Patty: How much did you lose?

Gamblers: I lost twenty-five thousand dollars and my friend got off easy and lost fifteen thousand dollars.

Patty: I was so outraged, you would have thought that all of the money was mind.

Both of my trick customers were staying at the Hard Rock Hotel, which symbolized to me their life. The Venetian was so cold, when they ran of of credit, the management told them "to leave and they would "comp" my customers next time they wanted to come to Vegas." I told my customer "never come back."

I picked up a couple at Bellagio's and took both of them to Paiute Golf Course. The cost of the ride was $48.80 cents. I remember it exactly. He gave me fifty dollars and asked me to come back, and pick him up. I thought to myself that "he would tip me later." I went back to Paiute, and on the way home, my fare was talking to his girl friend telling her about how much money he was making. Also, he was on his cell phone about his million dollar deals.

At Bellagio's, he tipped me another one dollar and eighty cents! One taxicab driver told me that he would not have let "Mr. Tightwad" out of his car. I remember once at Bellagio's, a customer had given a taxicab driver ten cents tip, and the driver threw it up against the wall.

One morning at the MGM, I picked up two Koreans, who could not speak very good English, they wanted to go to Primm Golf course, which is on the California,Nevada border. Joe, the doorman told them,"it is a long ride."

Koreans: We do not care.

Patty: We started of to Primm, I had my box lunch with me. When the fare got up to seventy-five dollars, I asked the Korean "who dreamed this one up." It ended up that MGM owned the golf course. They were so angry, that they told me,"we are going to call the MGM, and demand that the hotel send a limousine to pick us up."(They tipped me twenty dollars.)

Seventy dollars is such a good ride that every time, I would see Joe, I would ask him about giving me another ride to Primm.

I might add that a lot of people go to Primm, so it was not surprising that the MGM told the customers to go there. I am sure that the MGM told the Koreans that it was a long ride, because the MGM wants their customers to come back to Las Vegas and preferably to the MGM.

I had picked two Pakistanis in my car, and we were discussing world politics. When they got out of my car, they told me,"I was the most enlighten woman that they had ever met."

Patty: Have you ever talked to a woman before?

Pakistanis; No.

One day, my car just stopped at the Venetian Hotel right on Las Vegas Blvd. I was screaming to dispatch to get the tow truck to me. Frias only had one truck in service, which was not unusual. When the guys from Frias rolled up to me, they told me, YOU ARE OUT OF GAS. All drivers are suppose to put gas and oil into their cars at the end of their shift, I did not check my gas when I came on that morning. I gave each of the tow truck drivers ten dollars to say that my engine just stopped.

There is no rhyme or reason to the street names in Las Vegas. We have this huge book giving all of the directions in Vegas. At Yellow cab, they gave me ten pages of all of the streets that have changed their names. I just threw the new pages away. This makes me believe that the city planners are in the strip clubs getting drunk.

I understand Road Rage. When it is hot, and you are driving, it is very hard to hold your temper. If you miss a signal in Las Vegas, you are there for two minutes. I find myself yelling at the other drivers, "Move up, move up." At the airport, we have three lanes. one of them is our "go through lane." If I try too get over to the next lane to drop off, no one will give you a break. The cab drivers are always hitting someone or being hit by other taxicab drivers. (Including me.)

I picked up two different professional poker players. One had me drive him to a crummy apartment, and he tipped me around fifty cents.

Second gambler: I make so much money in Las Vegas that I can not afford not to return.

Patty: He left his luggage in my car, and when I brought it back to him, he "stiffed" me. I guess, "Nick the Greek," thought the fifty cents he had given me was sufficient.

We had a gaming convention in town, and I was talking to one of the conventioneers' and he told me, "any person that plays poker would not bring any attention to himself, and would act very humble." My fare also told me," I do not gamble, at all."

Patty: When people ask me where they should gamble, I always tell them to "stay in their rooms."

I picked up a man, and his wife at Mandalay Bay Hotel at nine thirty in the morning, and they wanted to go to the Flamingo Hotel. Forty-five minutes later, we had just gone five blocks, and their bill was around twenty dollars. Normally, we do not let people out except in designated areas, but it was wall-to wall traffic. I told my customers that it was against the law, but they could get out of my car, pay me, and walk the block to the Flamingo.

Both of the people got out of my car and a police officer ran over and told me, "it was against the law for them to get out."

Patty: What am I suppose to do, lock them in?

Police Officer: No, you are suppose to wave to me, and then I will run over and tell your customers that they are breaking the law for getting out of the car on Las Vegas Blvd.

Patty: They are from Cuba, and they do not understand English. It was true, but Mr. & Mrs. Carlos had lived in Florida for at least twenty years.

I had to say something or else the officer would have given me a ticket. There is a good reason for not letting people get out of your car on the street. If someone gets hit, the taxicab company is liable.

I picked up a customer from the Venetian Hotel and he told me how expensive food is in Las Vegas. "Dinners cost me about two or three hundred dollars."

Patty: Do you drink wine?

Fare: Yes, I do, and a bottle of wine starts at about sixty dollars.

Patty: Why don't you go over to a Seven-Eleven store, and buy your wine before you are going to eat at the Venetian. Later, I found out that the hotels can charge up to thirty dollars to open your wine.

I picked up a man from Switzerland, and he was going to Benions Horse Shoe downtown. I was talking to him about Switzerland's neutrality in all wars. I also asked him, "if it was true that you could go to Switzerland, buy drugs, and not go to jail?" "Yes." I was involved in the conversation and I missed the turn off on the freeway. (Buying drugs comes first.) By the time we arrived at the hotel, the bill was about seventeen dollars. He told me,"he understood,"and, he even tipped me.

Why Is South West Airlines the only airline that is making money? I was talking to a pilot and I told him, "it was because South West Airline does not penalize you when you change reservations." I flew into California and the fare was about one hundred dollars cheaper and no charge for the suit cases.

I had a customer who worked for a pharmaceutical company. I asked him, "why medicines are so expensive, and people have to go to Mexico or Canada to get their medicine?" John L. Lewis told me, "companies spend million of dollars developing a drug, and after all, the FDA could still turn it down."

A Japanese men was in my car,and I asked him if the "Japanese realize that "World War Two was started because of Pearl Harbor."

Nice Japanese Man: Yes

Patty: He was so funny.

Nice Japanese Man: We only bombed the United States once. We feel that it was dishonorable not to tell the Americans that we were going to war.

Patty: You feel It was alright, if Japan had declared war?

Nice Japanese Man: Yes.

FLASH: I had an elderly Japanese man in my car and he was "telling me how terrible Hiroshima was." It was all I could not say to him, "What about the rape of Nan King? All of the Englishmen you killed in Singapore? The Bataan March, and lets not forget Pearl Harbor." I kept my mouth shut for his fifty-cent tip. The Japanese are not noted for their tipping. I guess it is because in Japan, they do not tip, which is no excuse to me. When I go to a foreign country,

I try to find out the customs of the country. Of course, being an American, I tip everyone.

A Saudi was riding with me. (No matter what they say, they are married.) After we discussed OPEC and what we did for Saudi Arabia during the Gulf War, I asked him if his wife wore the veil. "Certainly," he replied. When I was in Egypt, I saw a women in a Babushka, and the material was very heavy. I asked him, "doesn't your wife get warm wearing one of those veils when the temperature is one hundred and eighteen?" He looked at me, and gestured, "Tough."

Patty: If a man had to wear one of those veils, the tradition would have ended yesterday.

I picked up a little boy, and his mother at the Venetian Hotel.

Patty: Sir, do you like Las Vegas?

Little Boy: I love it.

Patty: Do you enjoy the gambling?

Little Boy: No, but when I get older, I can gamble.

Patty: When we reached the Mandalay Hotel, he tipped me.

I picked up a stripper at the Crazy Horse Too, and she started crying. I asked her what was wrong?

Beautiful Dancer: I have not made a enough money to-night.

Patty; The owners take a percentage of money from the girls every night.

Beautiful Dancer: It is so cold in Crazy Horse too.

Patty: When a person drinks, they get very warm, so that is the reason why the gambling rooms, the strip clubs, and the bars are below 10 degrees.

Why don't you become a cocktail waitress.?

Beautiful Dancer: I am too old.

Patty: She was thirty-six and just gorgeous. Why don't you become a taxicab driver? An occupation that I would not wish on anyone.

Beautiful Dancer: I do not drive.

Patty: How did you do in school?

Beautiful Dancer; I was not a good student.

Patty; At this point, I just gave up.

One stripper from the Rhino Strip club was telling me, "I live with my boyfriend, and he doesn't make very much money. He would always take my money, but then he insults me about working at the Rhino."

Patty; Get rid of the bum.

I picked up another stripper that was going to college in Los Angeles. Probably, she was majoring in social services. She would come up to Las Vegas for a weekend and work at the Horse, and she would make two thousand dollars and then go home to continue her education. The smart stripper do not drink, or take drugs, but most of them get hung up with the wrong guy, drugs or liquor. I really do not want to sound condescending about the strippers, because I know how hard they work, and dealing with drunks all night long can add ten years to their lives.

CHAPTER FOUR
HOW I MAKE MONEY IN THE TAXICAB BUSINESS IN LAS VEGAS.

I have a number of way to make money in the taxicab business.

I always tell my customers that I have a speech problem so that they feel sorry for me. So, tip me.

Patty: I once talked to a foreign taxicab driver that was not doing well and I told the gentleman that he should say to all of his customers. "I have only been in the United Sates six months and I love America." Hopefully. they would ask him where he was from?

Al Beshir: I am from Darfur.

Patty: Since we deserted Darfur during their hour of need, the customer would feel guilty and tip him big." Al Beshir had too much pride or honesty to follow my word of wisdom.

Patty: How is the economy doing in your town, Elk Grove, Texas?

Elk Grove: Terrible

Patty: Las Vegas is dying on the vine. Customers always tell me that it is terrible since the September 11th bombing and now after the economy melt down. So, tip me.

I tell my customers when it's 118 degrees out, and people are walking in the heat, they are broke or masochistic. I use a four-syllable word to let my customers know that I am not dumb. So, tip me.

I aways tell my inmates, who are going to the MGM and the Hard Rock Hotel. "they are considered bad rides." When my customers ask me why? I reply, "the MGM, and the Hard Rock Hotel is too close to the airport." Let's not forget forget Motel Six. They usually laugh and give me a big tip.

Actually, I stayed at Motel Six when I first came to Las Vegas looking for a place to stay. Vegas now has such great fares, and hotel rooms,I would take the deals if I was going to go Las Vegas now.

The MGM, if you have a little bit more money, Bellagio's, and the Venetian.

If my customers are from Dallas, Jerry Jone's country, we talk football. The Texans usually denied that Mr. Jones is from Dallas. He really screwed up this time, what was the score, Philadelphia, 46, Dallas 6. It's just to bad, Bill Parcel is doing wonderful in Miami, although he lost in the play offs yesterday. I use to love it when Jimmy Johnson would tell Mr. Jones to get off the field.

When my riders are from Russia, I tell them that I was in Russia right after the fall of the Berlin wall. Most Russians, who have become citizens of the United States have no desire to go back to Russia ever to visit.

I always ask my customers if they need receipts? If they do, I always give my fares two extra receipts because I know that they have forgotten to ask their previous taxicab drivers. My fares always thank me, and let me know that the other drivers did not have my foresight.

I know that business expenses aren't what they used to be, when my Father was in business, you could declare everything, girl friends, dinners, and football tickets, etc.

When I have an Mexican man in my car, I always tell Jose that I lived in Mexico City, and Acapulco. American girls are considered bad girls in Mexico, and believe me, we were. I had so much fun in Mexico. I have never forgotten a drummer by the name of Tino Contreras. I always feel like going back to Mexico City, finding Mr. Contreras, and asking him if "he remembered me from thirty-five years ago. Mr. Contreras told me that, "he loved his drums, and women, and I do not know which came first.

If there are Mexican men in my car, and there aren't any women, "I tell my fares, that when I lived in Mexico, I used to say to my suitors, "Me sola, muey poko dinero, no estoy puta, which means, I am alone, I do not have very much money. I am not a whore."

I talked to a New Yorker who had moved to San Francisco. I asked him how he like the City, He replied, "I feel like a wolf in sheep clothing."

People from St. Louis, Missouri, I let them know that I use to work in Gas Light Square. At the time, all of the bars use to close at one-thirty in the morning, and we use to go to East St. Louis to drink.

CHAPTER FIVE
CORRUPTION IN THE TAXICAB BUSINESS LAS VEGAS.

In the next five chapters, I am telling the taxicab drivers side, but after the eighth chapter, I will come down on the drivers, very hard.

Las Vegas is the only major city in the world where you cannot own a cab or lease a taxicab. You have to work for someone else. Nine people control the taxicab business in Vegas.

Desert cab, Lucky Taxi, Western, and A-Cab are owned by one person. Four people own Yellow, Star and Checker Company, and my former boss, Charlie Frias owns Ace Cab, Vegas Vegas, Union, North Las Vegas, plus a limousine service. A family owns Henderson, Whittlesea, and a limo service. Of course, some of these taxicab owners have put their companies in other people's names, such as their wives, or the drunks down the street.

Mr. Frias has just started another taxicab company out in the boom docks called "Virgin Taxicab Co, and he said, "he wasn't making any money on this particular company."

Patty: Poor Baby.

My former boss, Charlie is eighty years old. He has no family, and he really needs all of this extra money, right?

Customers in the outer limits of Las Vegas do not usually take taxicabs. The Taxicab Authority lets Charlie bring in Virgin taxicab to Las Vegas. Later on, you will find out how significant this extra cab will affect the greedy cab owners.

Charlie Frias treats his taxicab drivers so badly that he will not talk to any of the drivers for fear of what, I dare not say! Well, he would not talk to me. Perhaps, he had heard of my bad driving. As you read this book, you will learn of the firing, and the people who were fired for no reason at all. To me, he is a real villain.

These owners are only allowed so many cabs per company. When the cab owners want more cabs, they just start another cab company, which means all of the other cab companies can acquires one more cab.

For all the advertising that is on a cab, the company receives around one thousand dollars per month. They have what is called a "wrap around cab." These cabs are painted to advertise one show, one hotel, all of the wonderful restaurants or where to go to get a piece of ass. These owners receive about two thousand dollars a month for this advertising

All of the taxicab companies receive about thirty cars from the car companies every year for testing. These cars are non gratis. (Free.)

We get a percentage of the money we bring in, plus our tips. A good day is about two hundred dollars. I do not care what Desert Cab says about their drivers bringing in over three hundred dollars a day, the drivers are turning tricks in the back seat of their cars.

One manager brought a friend of mine into his office, now this guy was a good driver. He was told that he would have to bring in more money to the taxicab company. My friend replied, "I have twenty-seven rides for the day."

Bad Manager: That is tough, you have to bring in more money or you will be fired.

This is an e-mail from Pancho:

You know George, the owner of Desert Cab got rid of me. Yeah, I made a lot of money on Friday, and when I dropped off, the girl told me that the owner wanted to talk to me. When I went into see George, he asked me about other cab companies and wanted me to spy for him.

George: You can get important information and numbers from the other companies because you write for the Trip sheet, and the Trip Sheet will give the information to you.

Pancho: No

George: I hate your fucking ass, and I could fire you when ever I want without any reason. I can fuck all of my drivers like Frias does, if I wanted too.

Pancho: I was out of there. What do you think?

Patty: I am now going to give you the "knock down," on how much money each cab company takes out of our checks everyday. At Frias, let's say that I have brought in two hundred dollars for the day:

Base Pay:	Two hundred dollars of which Frias takes one hundred dollars off of the top.
Gas Charge:	Two dollars a galleon, I use about 10 galleons. Twenty dollars a day.
Trip charge:	One dollar for twenty rides a day, twenty dollars.
Charles's run away money:	Four dollars, and fifty cents a day.

The amount comes to about comes to $145.50 dollars.

Dear Readers, do not forget, we have to pay our social security, and income taxes.

Everyday, I drove my cab, I knew that bastard was taking four dollars and fifty cents out of my check, and it put me in a rage. The Frias employees voted on a contract which stipulates that the employees give five dollars and fifty cents to Charlie everyday, and the drivers' voted for it, I am sure that the cabbies thought that the five dollars and fifty cents was for two beers that they would receive when the shift ended.

If a driver does not bring in enough money for the day, the supervisor makes the driver sign a "low booking sheet." One day, I was guilty of this crime, Bob, my supervisor at Yellow Cab, instructed me to sign the papers. I replied to Bob, "signing these documents is demoralizing, and just reinforces my own bad self image, can't you see how degrading this practice is for the drivers? I have been a bad girl, If you do not like my work, fire me, but do not make me sign any more of these sheets."

What am I suppose to do, if there are not enough customers out there in "Happy Land?" I cannot manufacture them. Do you want me to drive faster? I could have an accident, and I could be injured or killed along with my customer.

Patty: This leads to the practice of "long hauling," which I will explain later on.

At YCS, we have to wait a year and a half before we would get out benefits and at Frias, and Whittlesea, the taxicab drivers would have to wait for six months. I once called Desert Cab and asked them about their health benefits. Desert Cat told me that I had to work twelve hours a day, everyday for six months to get my benefits. We have more immigrants coming to America, and they cannot do anything to make money except drive a taxicab. The owners, naturally know this, and we had better not complain, if we want to keep out job.

On Christmas Eve of 2000, a taxicab driver who worked for Whittlesea, made a left hand turn on to Koval. A cab was coming south, the taxicab hit the on-coming car. The wife of one of the passengers was killed and her husband was in critical condition. It was said that liquor was involved. Naturally, the driver went to jail. After Law 101, I do not think that the plaintiff was drunk. If I am wrong about this, please call Pablo Cruz at Lucky cab.

I was talking to one of the drivers out at the "Pit," and I told him, "if it was me, I would own Whittlesea. The driver told me, "it will never happen." I assume that the driver meant that the taxicab companies have just a little bit of power, over the common man. me, the general public, and you.

Why do we work under these conditions? Before September 11th and the recession, all of us were making good money. The visitors did not come to Las Vegas after the bombing, you could have stayed at Bellagio's for ten dollars a night with an upgrade to a suite. O.K. Maybe thirty dollars a night. The drivers were not making any money.

Here is the part that kills me, the owners started putting more cabs out on the street.

Man does live by bread alone.

This is when I started hating the owners. I did not care if the drivers rolled the meter, or how much money they stole from the taxicab companies.

I was talking to a driver, and he told me that all of these owners are millionaires. God bless them. We are happy for all of the taxicab owners, but when they have become so rich that they are rolling money, they should try and make conditions for their people just a little bit nicer.

Exception: The owner of Lucky cab called his drivers in and said to the effect, "Let's all make money this year, and a little bit for me."

Patty: For this owner, I would die for, Paul Cruz, one of the great drivers in Las Vegas, has told me that the conditions at Lucky Cab are the best in Las Vegas.

The owners are so cheap, that they will not fill up the holes in the ground around the taxicab companies, and will not turn on the lights at three in the morning. It would be very easy to fall, and break your neck, better yet, a good lawsuit against the company.

www.vegascabbie.com is really just a place where Hound Dawg,(John Shannon) sits deciding who can put in their numerous E-mails on his site .He began to enjoy a little bit of too much power, and felt that he could be in collusion with the owners. Later on in my book, misery falls on John.

Whittlesea Cab Company fires Ray Stultz. Steve La Croix was trying to get Ray to file a grievance.

Ray posted this message in March.

"File a grievance with whom? The Steelworkers got me fired for saying something I didn't say The Steelworkers say that I was coercing drivers in the Pit, when I was picking up passengers at the airport. I was telling them to withdraw from the union and join the Professional Drivers Association.

Ray: I told Jim Lysengen when he called me into his office, that it is untrue and to call my accusers into the office.

Jim: Sheryl, the manager of Whittlesea said that the relationship wasn't going to work, and I have to let you go.

Ray: So, I asked Jim specifically, am I to understand that I am being terminated because I have told drivers to withdraw for the Union and join the Professional Drivers?

Jim: Yes, you can't discuss anything with company drivers except proper company business.

Patty: This means that Ray cannot be a member of the Elks Club. He also has to drop out of the charity which he funds for the Home of Pregnant Women. Also, you cannot be a member of the Union and the PDA.

Patty: Ray was talking to me about the next girl he was going to fuck.

All of the taxicab companies have different unions for their companies.

Patty: I have talked to different drivers that have said to me, "they have suits against their cab companies because they would not take care of the drivers after they have an accident or were robbed." One white driver told me " most of the immigrant drivers were afraid to say anything or to fight for their rights. The foreigner drivers probably thought that the police would drag them from their homes,

I mention that the driver was white, because they are the only ones that stick up for themselves.

I wanted to find out what the process is to buy a Las Vegas Taxicab. I also wanted to know how the owners would stop me from owning a cab.

I E-mailed Steve La Croix who answered me in July on my personal e-mail.

Steve: The requirements of applying for a certificate to operate a taxicab are outlined in NRS706.

The basic idea of the application is that you have to prove that there is a need for your service, and that your certificate operations would not adversely effect the other cab owners income.

Patty: In other wards, you would have to prove that you are not taking the food of of the plate of other owners?

At night time, the best rides are to the strip clubs, because they kick back to the drivers. The Doors were giving all of these rides to the limousines and then cutting it up with the Door. You can hear the screaming, and hollering through the ranks of the taxicab drivers. Darryl Poleman, who was the President of the PDA, and worked for Yellow Cab, put together a boycott at the Rio Hotel on a Saturday night between seven pm, and ten pm.

A little bit of back ground music, please. The Rio is off Las Vegas Blvd, to get down to the strip, you have to walk over the bridge, plus the railroad tracks. Can you imagine the women in their fur coats freezing in the wind. It was a cold night.

Jack said to me "Why make the tourists suffer?"

Patty: That is what striking is about.

After the boycott, all of cab companies received letters from the Rio Hotel telling us that "the doormen would no longer be able to ask customers where they were going too."

ON THE OTHER SIDE OF THE COIN

"Hot bodies, "posted in October by FN Cabbie on www. vegascabbie.com

Just a quick question? How many driers actually drop off at Hot Bodies knowing that it is a clip joint? For those that don't know the term,"clip joint" it stems from the fact that they basically take the customers money and toss them out the back door.

For instance, customer, Bob goes into Hot Bodies, Bob wants to see a girl so he pays about one hundred, and forty dollars to go into a room with a "clothed" woman to do some exercise. (Mind you, it's a health club now.) Bob is enticed by the girl to go further in their work out session. She tells Bob, "it's going to be X amount of dollars to go, "all the way with her," Bob agrees , and he gives the girl his credit card. While Bob waits in his room, the girl swipes the card for the agreed price. She comes back to the room to get Bob to sign for it, just so they can make sure that they get, "their money." The girl then leaves and she says she's going to slip into something more comfortable.

Shortly after the girl has left, "Big Bounce," enters the room and tells the customer that his time is up. Bob is naturally upset, because he paid for something he didn't get. "Big Bouncer," replies, "Sir, don't you know that prostitution is illegal in Clark County?" Then, out the door Bob goes. What's Bob to do?

Does he call the Better business Bureau? Does he call the cops? What can the cops do? Bob knows it's illegal to pay for sex in Clark County. If he tells (the cops) that he tried paying for sex, and got swindled, the cops will just laugh in his face. How does, Hot Bodies" stay in business, you might ask? Well, technically, they aren't breaking the law. They aren't selling sex, and there is no way to prove that Bob didn't get exactly what he paid for, a nice weight lifting session with a fully clothed woman for eight hundred dollars. She must be some trainer!

With this said, I do not take customers to Hot Bodies. Maybe, I have a bit more integrity as a driver, odd as that may sound. Don't you think its odd when a club charges the customer forty dollars, and gives you sixty dollars for bringing the customer to Hot Bodies?

But, more importantly, if they are giving you twenty dollars more than what they are getting, they have to get it back from the customer, or they are in a hole, with other clubs, what they give you is a wash. The customer pays twenty dollars, you get twenty dollars. The club doesn't lose money if the customer doesn't spend anything.

More power to all of you drivers that suggest a place like Hot Bodies, but when you take a customer to a place like Hot Bodies, it gives us all a bad name. I'm all for making money, but this is beyond the pale for me.

This is message that was sent to me over my personal E-mail.

Patty, I worry for you at this point, who will protect you? There are many items that can't be mention, but the trail of organized crime goes far beyond the city and all they way to the reaches of this county. The taxicab authority,the Governor, the agencies, and the government administrative bureaus, not to forget the Certificate Holders that have a well laid out scheme of an organized, controlled industry for the purpose of financial gain. This is a classic example of protectionism, and the R.I.C.O at its best, not to forget ANTI. Trust laws violations.

You must be very careful with whom you talk to or E-mail. You must be protected. I know people in this industry that have that data, and I would be willing to relay it, if they were protected by anonymity. I know that you have touched on the surface, on many issues, items, and occurrences, but it goes deeper than you know, and this could get people killed.

The corruption goes all the way from City Hall to the Governor, with the mob and the certificate holders in the middle."I look forward to reading your book."

Patty: I do not mind the corruption or that the owners are skimming off the top or how ever they make their money, I just feel that the taxicab drivers' should get a share of the pie too.

Dear Readers: notice the grammar and spelling. I will explain later.

This next message was posted on VC by Michael.

The Taxicab Authority was being asshole as usual. Hey Plunkett, I thought you said on the radio they don't act like that yen right yeah fucking lie anyway he says did she get into your cab I said Ya and she gave me one hundred dollarsstto do it shit, I don't gave a fuck one hudred dollrs you in, but anyway,

TaxiCab Authority being smart ass says stay her and walks away with Tony my supervisor and and they have in a good ol time with all the doormen and security so, when they were done with the pow-wor the taxicab authority comes over and say I ave wrinted you a pink slip im like shy for f.r.o.n. l.o.a.din.g that's way and I am thinking to myself she was a personal what do you want me to bloc the the fucking limo land so Icna find here thought it used common sensewith this but guess what Im cab driver im at fault to just appling for the job it's like when you get robbed it's your fault no oe els bullwhip. Your not the wrong the mother fucker who robbed you is what did you sayo.k....Put that guy to my and oh, there take my money and here my wedding rign and oh, ya, here is my lic just so you know where I live comeone this is bullshit the Taxi Cab Authority don't take you side of the story for shit why because you in he wrong from the start

ok look now many times are we going to here dave Taxi Cab Authority tells us in class come on guys use your heads be smart well if we new the out come of the ride dave all be rich and there would be no robbers so in cast Taxi Cab authorty don't listed to me once diden't ask me shit and wrote didn't listed to me once.

Diden't ask me shit and wrote a pinke and said to what about the doormen and what not for detain me that's got to be against the law, the Taxi Cab Authority answer is I told them they can't do that is aginst the law and they came take your permit eather ok so why are you givein me this pink slip im ot sure if they roke the law and I did to picin up a personal where his ticket or there tickets since im a cabbie im in the wrong and thes doormen there rightok the law bend for them but not for me I have every right to e mdd a this and the Taxi Cab Authority say trust uswell how can I when I'm treated like this no repect.

Patty: Michael's spelling is worst then mine. I would never let it get this far with the doormen, I would have talked to the Door,and explained the situation, and I would comment on how hard they work, because they do, and ask for permission to get in line. Otherwise, I would have waited to see if my customer was going to come out.

I do not know how many of you have watched the series on television called, "Sanford and Son." There is a crime in the neighborhood and a black police officer, and the white policeman comes over to question Sanford. The white police officers talked in a different language, English, that Sanford could not understand. The black officer interprets everything to Sanford.

I will try to interpret this last message for you.

Michael: I am a Yellow Cab Driver, and my cab number is 1781. Most of you know me, and I am sure you've heard this story.

I was at the Palm's Hotel to pick up a client, and she wasn't there. So, I though, I would get into line to pick up someone else, if she did not show up. I was surprised to see my original customer, and she got into my cab. She gave me a hundred dollars and told me to hurry up as her feet are killing her. I move out of the line with her. The doorman runs up to me, and he tells me, "I am jumping out of the line."

So, Amy the girl I had picked up, said,"she was sorry for all of the bullshit," left me the hundred dollars and left for finer greenery.

Patty: Why don't I get these hundred dollar customers?

Michael; The security guard opened my door, and took my permit, and calls the taxicab authority.

Patty: It seems that the supervisor could have resolved this problem with out calling the fucking useless TA. Once I was at the Venetian and a customer jumped in my cab out of line, I told the doormen that "I was sorry," and he let it go.

Michael calls his supervisor, and he shows up,at the same time as the TA arrived. Mike's supervisor, and the TA were both talking to him. The TA official tells Mike, they are giving him a pink slip for "front loading."

Patty: The rest of this message is Michael just talking about the trials and sufferings of being a taxicab driver.

Hound Dawg posted this message to Michael on September 24[th.]

I have decided to ban Michael, taxicab number 781, the Scripture," from the board. I do so with regret as I think Michael is a nice person, however, the pointless form of posting, he's using does nothing but tell the rest of the readers of this site that we are no better than a bunch of 21st century cave men. I am leaving his posts on the board as a example of what kind of poor taste with gets you booted from here.

Patty: Michael does not use the "King's English" to express himself. So, it is a crime to be illiterate. Actually, illiteracy in men or women become a bore with time. Illiterately shows that person does not have a very good vocabulary. I really feel that Michael was putting us all on, because I know that he was much smarter and only used his writing to make a point.

Patty: I am outraged about Bill Shranko using every power at hand to get rid of www.vegascabbie.com. Bill Shranko drove a cab for fifteen years, and then he was fired from Whittlesea Cab Company. I had heard that he had a heart attack at Whittlesea, and Whittlesea with all of its honor intact, fired Bill.

As Capitan of the ship at Yellow Cab, you would think Bill would have some insight and understanding of the problems that the taxicab drivers have to go through everyday. I feel that all Bill wanted was just to have drivers come to work, and not cause any problems. Who can blame him?

CHAPTER SIX
THIS MEANS WAR

About seven of the strip clubs have decided not to tip the taxicab drivers. These clubs are, the Olympic Gardens, the Spearmint, Rhino, the Club Paradise, Cheetahs, Deja Vu, and the Crazy Horse Too. Mr. Eliades owns the Olympic Gardens Strip Club, as well as a quarter of interest in Yellow, Checker, and Star Taxicab company. Pete had started a lawsuit to stop the tipping to the drivers. Therefore, the taxicab drivers have refused to pick up at his club.

Before Pete started this law suit, I dropped off at the Olympic Gardens. I did not know if I was supposed to get a gratuity for the ride or not. I went in and asked for the manager about the money. He started to push me away, telling me, "to get out."

Patty: Hey, I am a taxicab driver, not one of your girls. Next time I will take my customers to the Crazy Hose, which is a better strip club.

Mr. Eliades has said and I am quoting him now, "In the last two years, I have given the taxicab drivers more then two million dollars."

Patty: If this is true, Pete has had two thousand, seven, hundred sixty-two people in his club every day. This seems like a lot of customers to me, and Mr. Eliades should be rolling in money. What kills me is that Pete drove a cab for fourteen years in Las Vegas.

The girls that work at these clubs are a very cheap commodity to the owners. Mike Tyson was in Cheetahs, and one of the strippers came up to say hello to Michael, or wanted to talk to him. He pushed her away, HARD. She was fired, and she started a lawsuit against Mike Tyson. I do not understand what is wrong with Michael, it probably had something to do with cocaine. I definitely feel that he needs a Nanny.

Jeff German wrote this article on April 12, 2002 with this Las Vegas Sun newspaper.

ELIADES BRNGS FIGHT TO CABBIES.

Las Vegas cabbies should have learned by now not to underestimate Pete Eliades, the outspoken Olympic Gardens Club Owner, who is not holding back any punches in his high stake battles with drivers unlawfully diverting passengers away from his popular topless night club.

Eliades raised the stakes last week,when he filed a racketeering lawsuit, alleging cabbies were conspiring with the manager of the rival Palomino Club to steal thousands of dollars in business from him each night. "I filed the lawsuit to stop the bleeding," Eliades says. I am not going to quit fighting until the cabbies stop cheating the public. I want to eliminate the crooks."

Patty: I have heard that he might start with himself.

Jeff: Eliades alleges that drivers have been paid fifteen dollars to twenty dollars a head to divert passenger to the all-nude Palomino Club seven miles down the street. The Palomino Club immediately stopped giving drivers cash as a sign of good faith. This quick move underscored the seriousness of the civil racketeering allegations leveled in the suit, put together by attorney, Dominic Gentile who once chaired the American Bar Association Racketeering Cases Committee. These charges are modeled after the criminal laws, congress passed more than thirty years ago to fight the nations organized crime families.

Patty: It seems the racketeering committee missed a few people.

Palomino Club manager, according to Eliades, have engaged in a pattern of unlawful activity for months to hurt the Olympic Gardens Club business and to obtain money from the public under false pretenses. He says that passengers taken to the Palomino Club have not been told that all or part of their twenty dollar admission fee is being returned to the cabbies.

What Eliades has done by filing this complaint is to demonstrate that he's not going to roll over and play dead for the cabbies, who also have tried to put a dent in his business by staging a mean-spirited boycott of the Olympic Strip Club.

Nearly three hundred unidentified cabbies and supervisors from the thirty local companies have been dragged into the conspiracy as defendants in the suit. Elide and Gentile plan to identify those defendants in the coming weeks and proceed with the case against them, even if a deal is reached with the Palomino managers.

The suit already has stirred up the chat line on www.vegascabbie.com, a website for local drivers. Much of the talk, surprisingly, has been critical of Eliades.

"I am patient logical individual who believes in the the rule of common sense,"writes John Shannon, who runs the web site." This new action defies both logic and common sense." Another driver, Raymond R. Stultz, adds, "No one can justify this type of action or attack on the hard working low-paid ambassadors of this city.

Patty: As far as being low paid, I have never made so much money in my whole life, and I left a good computer job in San Francisco.

Jeff: We can expect the anger level to remain high as the suit proceeds against the cabbies reported to be diverting passages away from the Olympic Gardens.

Life can become uncomfortable for these driver, especially if John Plunkett, the Administrator of the State Taxicab Authority,takes an interest in the racketeering case.

Even bigger shocks waves could rumble through the taxicab industry if Eliades can prove that the cab company supervisors allowed the conspiracy against him to thrive without taking actions against their own drivers. This could jeopardize the operating certificates of the companies, even those owned by Yellow, Checker, and Star Transportation where Eliades has a financial interest. Eliades, it would seem is someone you do not want to underestimate.

Patty: I really had visions of Pete Eliades serving the Frias Company, a subpoena, I thought to myself, "Pete would not be able to frighten Charlie." I went into work today and there was sign on the bulletin board informing all of the drivers that we had to sign a form saying if we did not pick up at the Olympic Gardens, or if we diverted customers to another club, we would be fired! Now, understand, we had to sign these papers, or we would not be able to get our checks. I expected Frias to tell Pete to go to hell, frankly, I was disappointed

During this atrocious time, the Olympic Gardens was busted for charging at the door for gambling and prostitution. He was also charged for allowing his name to be used on a pornographic website. Six dancers were arrested for prostitution.

Yolanda posted in August on www.vegascabbie.com

I feel that it was very upstanding of Pete to fire these girls, as if he didn't know what was going on. I do not know exactly what happened, but I seriously doubt if the Olympic Garden Strip Club ever discouraged this type of behavior before.

With Pete's statement, Sometimes, they get carried away, that tells you, Pete was aware of what was going on in his club.

Patty: I have heard, "a little taste for himself."

Yolanda: But, he is all right now, and the girls are unemployed. Whatta guy! Don't these girls even get a fair trial before they are fired? I am sure if Pete used one of his high priced attorneys he could get the court to believe that they were nuns.

But, obviously, he has the same respect for his dancers as he has for cab drivers. Just goes to show his true colors, as if everyone but his family knows it.

Patty: When Pete was driving a cab (before Christ), he was out there hustling just like all of us picking up his two dollars or five dollars from the Palomino Club. Mr. Eliades was on Hound Dawg, radio show, www.vegascabbie.com, He was talking about how honest he is in his public dealings. Pete is upset that the other cubs are paying the taxicab driver's more money then the Olympic Garden. I almost threw up when he said ,"the public is being robbed." Pete made the remark, he did not know how the taxicab drivers can go home and face their families.

I always tell my Customers to stay out of strip clubs. If my fares insists that they want to go to the clubs, that is their problem.

This article was posted on April 5, 2002 by Jeff German of the Las Vegas Sun Newspaper.

TAXICAB AUTHORITY CHIEF HAS HIS HANDS FULL.

Dear Readers, you will love this post. I never realized that Jeff had such a great sense of humor, maybe because he just written a book about the Binion murder in Las Vegas. It is called, "Murder in Sin City."

Jeff: Life is anything but boring inside the colorful Las Vegas taxicab industry. Former FBI Agent John Plunkett, who is running the State Taxicab Authority is finding out that after eight months on the job, that he would rather be a barker at one of the casinos. Plunkett spent most of his career in- law enforcement chasing mobster, drug dealers, and crooked politicians.

Today he's working for the taxicab owners that reap the benefits of the crooked drivers they employ whom illegally rip off customers by taking the long route. He is also in the middle of a high-stakes kicked back war between topless nightclubs bribing cabbies to bring tourists to the clip joints so they can be ripped off before they lose all of their money gambling.

His work may not be as dangerous now, but it's much more profitable and Plunkett seems to be adapting to it with the ferocity and devotion as with his days with the FBI. There is a feeling within the industry that Plunkett, with his even-handed style and law enforcement mentality, has the potential to become the wealthiest Taxicab Authority Administrator in the agency's thirty-two year history. He doesn't play favorites with the topless bars he visits, or with the kickbacks, he receives.

Lately, however, his job has brought home a few new problems. Puckett's biggest source of income has been the Olympic Gardens Strip Cub Owner, Pete Eliades, who is on a relentless anti-diversion campaign and worse topless club is one of the cities worst clip joints, some of his better-known competitors concur. The cabbies have tried to warn customers to stay away from the Gardens. Eliades filed suit against the better topless clip joints earlier this year to stop them from telling the truth about his lousy place of business.

This goaded Eliades into stepping up his campaign against the cabbies. Recently, Eliades spent a weekend visiting the better clip joints, where drivers are telling visitors to go. He jotted down the breast sizes and names of the dozens of beautiful strippers that refuse to work at his club. His list found its way to Plunkett, who knows it's against Taxicab authority regulations for strippers to decline giving oral sex.

Eliades and his Attorney have also been keeping track of dozens of ugly dancers who work at the Olympic Gardens. One night last weekend, Eliades came to the doorstep of The Palomino club in North las Vegas, his latest rival, looking and trying to learn how they might lure some of these beautiful strippers to work for his topless strip joint. He was offering strippers up to twenty dollars for their pictures. That night dancers were milling around the parking lot and lining up to receive their cash, while tourists at major strip resorts, were told, "We are having a tough time finding a good piece of ass for you" There's something wrong with that scenario.

Plunkett says he is doing everything within his power to stop Eliades (from) giving his money to the strippers and giving it to him instead. He has been conducting personality classes and a manners class to all the bad apples that he employs for two months and plans to make it a regular practice, but Plunkett explains, he doesn't have to go thru all of that. He told Eliades to make sure all of his ugly dancers and rude personnel should be fired. But he says, this is the responsibility of the thug supervisors that work for him.

Plunkett's biggest problem on the street is not only catering to Eliades, nor even stopping prostitution, but rather from preventing dancers from turning tricks in the parking lot of the Garden's Club. His customers feel when they are looking for a prostitute, they should at least be halfway good looking. public is really getting screwed here, he says. When you talk to Plunkett, you can tell he needs all the help he can get to deal with Eliades sorry clip joint. Finding a good prostitute is growing problem. You can tell his job isn't boring."

Patty: I was telling one of the taxicab drivers, and I was telling him what a wonderful guy Bill Shranko is to me. I felt that he was such a good, straight man. I was talking to Bill and I said to him," the name of the game is money." he said to me, "Honest money, Gretchen."

Driver: One of these days, you will find our all he cares about is himself.

Patty; I understand how Bill feels, because it is the right way to be in the taxicab business in Las Vegas, since it is for sure that no one else gives a damn about you.

This fax was set to Bill Shranko, the manger of YCS. This is his reply to questions from John, and Diane Shannon, it was posted on www.vegascabbie.com

Dawg: Are we requiring drivers to pick up customers who are waiting after drivers drop them off at the Olympic Gardens Strip Club?

Bill: Yes, we are, in addition, this includes any other places including Bellagio's, Caesars, and the Palomino or any other customers who have loads waiting.

John: Are we requiring drivers to stage at the Olympic Gardens Club with a line of cabs already on the stand and does not have customers waiting?

Bill: No.

John: Have we done this before?

Bill: Yes. At every airport boycott many times, and the Rio Hotel boycott, at the Mandalay Bay Hotel, and New York, New York Hotel boycott, and at every other place of business that may have been waiting.

John: Have we gone to other cab stands where there are no loads, and many cars are staging, and assigned them to service customers waiting at other locations?

Bill: You bet your life that we have, and we will continue to do this. The real laws you know, the ones that are written are very clear. Certificate are required to provide service to customers, or we can face loss of our certificate to operate. That's why boycotts are not legal.

Patty; Who writes up these laws? Isn't this ridiculous. Taxicabs drivers are not in the same category as brain surgeons or air controllers. We should be able to strike. It would just be too damn bad if some of these owners lost their certificates, and had to give up one of their cab companies.

Bill: I guess what really bother me is that no one even seems to say anything about the reasons we are all here, the companies, the drivers and the Taxicab Authority. We here to service the customers.

Our purpose is not to boycott the airport, hotels, businesses, or casinos but simply show all of our visitors that they will get a safe ride and make them realize that we are delighted that they came to Las Vegas, and we want them to come back very soon.

Thousands of our drivers in this community are hard working, honest, and totally devoted in doing a professional job each, and every day. Thirty or forty drivers are the unhappy souls,no matter where the are. They simply exist to start confrontations,and never have a nice word to say about anyone. Their entire life is based on negativity and they are ripping customers off. They do not have the courage to use their real names.

They don't care about ruining the reputation of their fellow drivers. They could care less about treating our visitors with class. If they really cared about their fellow drivers, the thirty or so malcontents would have crawled out of their sewers to attend the recent TA workshop. This was a discussion of the important tipping issue, supposedly of concern to all drivers.

It would have been good for taxicab drivers to show up at this meeting. The total amount of drivers attending was zero. You can count the John Shannon's, Craig Harris, or impetus Ruthie Jones, because they are at every meeting doing what they do best. Who else was there? Milton Schwartz, and I were representing YCS. Milton did a wonderful job of representing our position in supporting repeal of the language prohibiting tipping. YCS, Checker and Star were the only company to publically take that position in support of the drivers.

Patty: Instead of Hound Dawg representing us, it should be the union.

Bill: Has anyone called to thank us? Has anyone of the anonymous malcontents called, and thanked us, or at least said they they appreciated our support? Of course not. These fools are not happy unless they make everyone else unhappy.

Steve La Croix, who has the courage to use his name, and I have put our differences aside to work together on behalf of the drivers. Ruthie Jones, John, and Diane Shannon were also there. Craig Harris is always working for the drivers. They do not hide behind a fabricated name, and they always get things done.

Patty: These people who go to these meeting must "get off," in some way.

Bill: The Trip Sheet was correct. Sometimes a drivers worst enemy is himself. Or, as I have said many times, "There are some drivers who delight in killing the goose that laid the golden egg. Well, John Shannon, and Diane, I'm too busy at YCS trying to manage thirteen hundred of the best drivers in the Industry. I may not be able to respond regularly, but I'll try when I can. I've already accepted your invitation to appear on your radio show and I am looking forward to it."

In the meantime, if anyone in the industry wants to find out the truth on any subject, I'm always available monthly at the Taxicab Authority meeting, and I have never turned down a union invitation or a PDA invitation, and I also always use my correct name.

Patty: And, with that, Bill wraps himself in the American flag.

Mr. Swartz, one of the owners held a vote to repeal the law suit. Without Pete it would have been three to one. Pete decided that he would go for the four to zero.

Patty: I talked to a cab driver that had been driving a cab for twenty years, and he apparently knows Mr. Eliades. He told me, "Mr. Eliades is the nicest person away from the taxicab business, if you have a problem, Pete will be there for you "in a New York minute."

Pete trying to help you is like the executioner who is showing you the way to the gallows. I cannot stand people who not consistent in their personalities.

I asked the driver,"Would you forget your roots if you were in Pete shoes? "Would you still care about the taxicab drivers?"

Cab Driver: No.

Patty: That about sums it up as far as loyalty goes in the taxicab business. It is hard work, and when a cab driver manages to get a supervisory job, he loves it, because he no longer has to work twelve hour a day.

The Dawg posted this message on his site.

News from the Olympic Gardens Strip Club.

Pete Eliades has announced through Bill Shranko that the Olympic Gardens Strip Club will begin accepting passes from other adult night clubs.

Patty: The Palomino wanted out of the law suit, and they said something, to the fact that they were on the side of Pete. This is so much bullshit, the Palomino was making nothing but money during this tipping conspiracy. Who would go to the Palomino Club, it is so far north on the strip, that it almost touches Utah.

At one point, the lawyers for Pete said "the Palomino Club would have to open it's books."

Patty: I would love to see Pete's books, and not the ones that he shows to the IRS. Recently, Mr. Eliades opened a new nightclub called the Sapphire Strip Road.

Hound Dawg posted this message in June on VC.

Before you cheer for the possible demise of Pete Eliades, keep one thing in mind; Tratos saw no problem with the doormen at Sapphire diverting cab loads to the house limos.

Patty: This is so typical of a taxicab drivers mentality, because one boss lets the doormen divert cab loads to the limousines, they will take any amount of shit that is handed to them by Pete Eliades.

In The Year Of Our Lord:2008, the drivers now get seventy dollars from Can,Can Room, and fifty dollars from all of the other strip clubs. Not bad!

I was not involved with Bill during all of this "tip number." All I know is that he was wonderful to me. I hope that he is well and happy.

CHAPTER SEVEN
TAXICAB AUTHORITY

This next letter I wrote to the Governor about the taxicab authority.

To: Governor K. Guinn

555 East Washington Ave.

Suite 5100

Las Vegas, Nevada 89147

From: Patty Noland

Regarding: Incident on Wednesday September 26th.

Dear Sir:

This is in essence of what I wrote to Mr. Plunkett, head of the Taxicab authority.

On Wednesday, I was at the airport and a customer got into my cab. He had to walk down to number two, which can be a long walk. He was angry. I asked him where he wanted to go?

He told me Spencer Street. I told him that I would go down Tropicana to Spencer Street He told me, "no," and stated that he wanted to go down to Swenson, turn on Twain and then go to Spencer Street.

Patty: What is wrong?

Son of Sam: Fuck you.

Patty: Who do you think that you are talking too?

Son of Sam: I have no qualms about hitting you in the face or kicking in your head.

Patty: I made a right on Tropicana, and went to the first gas station and told Sam, "your ride with me is over with, and get out of my cab."

Son of Sam: I will get out of your taxicab if you will call me another cab.

Patty: Since I will to pay for your fare that you have run up, I will not drop a dime for you.

Natalie Inferno from the TA came to investigate. At the airport, I had put the time, the number of passengers, and the destination, but I had not finished my trip sheet. It wouldn't have been that difficult for me to figure out how much Son of Sam's ride had cost. Since I was thinking about someone kicking me in the head, I was hardly worrying about Union Cab making money, at this point of the game.

The customer was as calm as a cucumber, while I was very upset. From her observation, Natalie said, "I was probably in the wrong, because the customer was so polite."

Patty: I can't believe how stupid it was for her to say that to me. To me, this means the customer have had more experience with the police that I have.

Natalie then told me that the customer could take any taxicab that they wanted at the airport, but that was not the dispute, Sam got into my car, "happy, well, maybe angry, I don't know." I hope that he wasn't so furious to take it out on more defenseless me.

The airport police have all of the cabs lined up to keep the airport running smoothly. I asked one of the police, if a customer can pick and choose what cab, they want to take in the line. He nearly flipped out and said something to the affect that "Natalie should stay off of their turf."

Apparently, I said something or interrupted or overstepped my position. I honestly do not remember that I had insulted her in any way. If I had insulted her, that's just to bad.

Natalie told me that she was there for me, if this was true, I told her,"she could speak to me more politely." Natalie feels that if she talks tough, she can be one of the boys.

Natalie was not concerned about the man threatening me, but she was more interested in the dress I was wearing. When she called my supervisor, she told him that I was not wearing a bra, and that I was in my night gown. I wear long dresses that cost a lot of money.

The only reason I wear these dresses is because my weight fluctuates between one hundred and thirty pounds too one hundred sixty pounds. I am at the wrong end of the scale right now. I was in a very expensive white dress, and I must have leaned against the wall with a coke which left a mark on my dress. Maybe thirty years ago, I would have gone to work without a bra, but not now.

I am outraged by the way she has treated me, I would like to have some sort of meeting with Natalie, because she is not qualified to be TA police officer.

Son of Sam should have been arrested. If I had called the police, Sam would have gone to jail. I would like to think of the Taxicab authority being there for the drivers, but I must tell you, that all of the drivers hate the TA, and they know that they cannot depend on your organization for anything. I have written letter of appreciation to the airport police and to the convention traffic police, who have a thankless job as far as I am concerned, because they always try to help me.

I know that Natalie is not trying to win a popularity award, but all of the doormen, and the drivers to whom I talked to cannot stand Natalie. I might also add that I am not just a loose cannon out there. All the doormen are wonderful to me, they know that I have arthritis, and they all load the cars for me. I have a speech problem, and Natalie kept asking me if I was loaded. I also have a hearing problem, and I am certified as a disabled person.

When Natalie told me that if I had "just shut the fuck up, everything would have been alright," I could not believe it. I do not need the word "fuck" to express myself, and I do not see why I should accept it from someone else. If I have another encounter with Natalie, believe me, I will be ready for her verbally, and I know that I am above her intellectually.

Patty Noland

Patty: After Natalie talked to my boss, and I returned to the office, I was almost fired by my, "Give me another ten dollars" immediate boss, who had the nerve to say to me that Union Cab takes too good of care of me.

Patty: What about all of the ten, and twenty dollars that I have given to you?

Jack stepped in and suspended me for three days. At first I thought, goody, goody for me, I can go home, and work on my computer The longer I thought about it, I wondered why I was suspended in the first place.

Amigo: My friend Amigo, was in his cab downtown. A lady approached him with a suitcase, and Amigo thought she was going to get into his cab. Instead, she just put down her suitcase on the ground, and then just laid down, and went to sleep.

Along comes our heroine Lucy Lick A Lot from the TA, she yells at Amigo, "Why is your car pulled out from the curb?"

Patty: You can see that this is probably the most important issue of the day, and the TA has to deal with this crises.

Amigo: Go around the car and see the woman.

Lucy starts kicking the woman to wake her up.

Amigo: It is not right to kick her.

Lucy: Amigo, you leave the taxi stand, because it isn't any of your business.

This next message was posted by an airport policeman and was posted on VC.

Today, I was working the departure curb at the airport, and a NLV taxicab came to my attention. It was parked across the sidewalk and causing a commotion with all the people trying to cross over the street. The driver was busy unloading the taxi, so I decided to wait for him to finish, and than I planned to mention to him that it would be better to unload his passengers on the curb away from the cross walk.

While I was waiting for him, I noticed he had the green light emergency light on! I quietly asked him if everything was all right. He said, "Yes" and continued to unload leaving the light on.

At this point, I thought I was dealing with someone that did not know about the crosswalks and must have made a mistake and activated the light by accident. I had no intention of doing anything except just telling him to be careful.

After his passengers left I asked him why his emergency light was on. He told me (in poor English) he had intentionally put it on because he felt it was good to have the flashers on when he stopped at a curb. I explained to him that he should only use this light when someone has a gun to his head. I pointed to the taxi lights to show him which light to activate if he wants the flashers on. The driver said he is NOT a beginner, I cannot understand how he could not be better informed.

Of all the tickets, I hate to write is the ones that go to the taxicab drivers. I go for months without needing to cite a taxicab driver. (THIS ONE GOT THE TICKET.) I have never cited anyone for blocking a cross walk before. My hope was that this citation would force him to understand his responsibilities better.

I hope it will be a long time before the next citation is needed.

LONG HAULING

1

This article was in the Las Vegas Mercury sometime in 2002 by Mr. George Knapp.

The name of the piece is, "Taxicab accent becomes impenetrable during fare dispute."

When I e-mailed Mr. Schumacher, who is the editor, he replied to me "you must realize, I assume, that this is a work of satire. It must be characterized as such and we must get full credit for the work."

Patty: It might be a satire, but, I am sure it happens all of the time.

Though he spoke nearly perfect and barely inflected English on the drive from the airport, taxicab driver's Behrouz became a dense thicket of barely recognizable grunts and shouts during a fare dispute in the Bellagio's driveway Saturday morning.

Lari had barely picked up tourists Clay, and Diane Poshok from McCarran airport, he began a rambling but perfectly understandable, monologue about the cities many attractions.. When hearing the Poshoks were staying at the Bellagio's, Lari even recommended that the couple see "the exquisite Dale Chilhuly exhibition."

But, relations soured when Mr. Clay Poshok offered a fifty-dollar bill for a twenty dollar fare. As Poshok waited for the change, Laris's grasp of the English language inexplicably faltered. Stumped for the exact phrase, Lari began slamming his open palm against the dashboard, and was screaming. "Nochain,nochain."

2

Dear readers, there are reasons all of the cab driver's believed Mr. Schumacher article is it a common practice of some of the taxicab drivers. Mark, you are the only honest cab driver left in town.

A cab driver picked up a woman at the airport. She wanted to go to the Treasure Island Hotel, and without asking her if she wanted to go the fast way which would cost her more money, the driver was all over the board. She called her husband over the cell phone, she told him that "she did not where she was going." her husband told his wife to pay the usual price which is about twelve dollars.

When she got our of the car, she told the doorman what she was doing. He back her completely. The cab driver started yelling at the Door telling him to go, "fuck" himself."

CHAPTER EIGHT
LONG HAULING FUN

Among some other businesses I own is a small (50-taxi) cab company in a large market. I come to Las Vegas once or twice a year for a little R&R and to unload excess profits.

A buddy of mine, and I come to Vegas in June of this year, and we thought that just for the fun of it, we should check out this "long haul" business." I had read about the long hauling from the airport to the strip. Rather than renting a car at the airport, and paying the 10% airport surcharge, we decided to catch a cab to the Strip, and pick up a car at our hotel I figured most drivers were legit, and we probably would get taken the short way and just have a good conversation with the driver and give him twenty dollars for the ten-dollar ride.

Well, we hooked a real live one, a white guy with, curly black hair, I think it was a Whittlesea cab, but I do not remember. So, my buddy told the driver, "Caesar Palace, and take the shortest way." The driver says, "Ya, man, no traffic lights this way." So, he goes past the Flamingo Road exit to the Spring Road, and then turns off and heads back south on the Strip to Caesar's.

The meter was just under twenty dollars I told the guy to pull over outside of Caesar's Hotel. I handed the guy nine dollars, and told him to keep the change.

3

He starts yelling that the meter (read) nineteen dollars and something, I laughed, and said, "Hey, Buddy, stuff it up your thieving ass." He jumped out of his cab as if he was going to fight my buddy and me. We are both over six feet tall, and weigh over two hundred and twenty five pounds.

So, he starts screaming that he is going to call the cops. I laughed, and said to him, "Don't bother, I'm calling the Taxicab authority now to report you for long hauling." When he saw the cell phone in my hand, he got back in his cab, yelled a string of obscenities, and burned out. almost smashing into a another cab.

Love your city. See you in December.

Patty: Every taxicab driver who is white, and has curly hair at Whittlesea, has now dyed their hair blond and have made a trip to the beauty salon to have their hair straightened.

I picked up a couple from Bellagio's Hotel, I was taking them to the airport. My fares were two Japanese and a baby, just the profile that thieving drivers' wanted to take to their hotel. My fare was only twelve dollars, their fare to Bellagio's was twenty five dollars. I mention this to another driver and he was happy because he had given Pautu a ride, and Pautu did not tip him.

A customers told me that he wanted to go to the Stardust Hotel, so I started for the freeway he told me to "back up" right on the freeway that leaves from the airport. Carl said to me, "if I took him through the tunnel, it would eat up my tip." Needless, to say, I was embarrassed and I would have been a hell of a lot more embarrassed, if the TA stopped me for backing up on the the airport exit.

I asked one of my favorite drivers, if you ever long haul fares to the MGM.

Fast driver: If I don't like them, I do.

CHAPTER NINE
DANGER IN THE TAXICAB BUSINESS IN LAS VEGAS.

4

I love Las Vegas. The security this town has for cab drivers is unbelievable.

At the Stratosphere Hotel on the strip, a man, and a woman went into a room, where they robbed and strangled a visitor to death. These murders walked out into the hallway. John, and his wife were on camera, and the next day, they were both arrested.

Apparently, when Steve La Croix was president of the Professional Driver's Association, this accident happened.

Rodney L. Johnson posted this message in August.

Steve, yes, I was hit in Vegas on Las Vegas boulevard going north in the far left lane. One of your upstanding individuals came tearing out the Sahara hotel parking lot, crossed three lanes of traffic, and T-boned me. My 2001, Harley-Davidson was totaled. I incurred the following injuries; broken left rib, which punctured my lung. Bachia Plexus area crushed, hence, I now hare a paralyzed left arm. My left leg was broken, and my right leg was severely sprained. I also incurred a right knee injury. This was all caught on camera by the Sahara Hotel's surveillance camera.

Patty: All drivers turn north on Las Vegas Blvd, to make a quick turn. I once took a woman "the right way, behind the hotel, and she accused me of long hauling her."

Mr. Johnson: Before you run off at the mouth, you had better put your little pea-sized brain in your ear. You do not call my integrity in question ever. I see you cabbies drive and the rude manner in which you drive. I really don't care about your financial situation or how much money you make. As long as you're out there, I see a menace on the road Rude behavior, cutting off or just flagrant driving which all leads to one thing, my going after your job. Oh, by the way, jerk off, before you call someone a coward, you should check his or her background.

However, as I am dealing with the dregs of society, I do not believe it is necessary to reveal my record of service in Vietnam to you. Oh, just for your own edification, you do know what edification means, don't you?

5

Patty: I do not particularly like being called a dreg of society, scum is more like it.

I picked up a fare who told me, "I need to go to an ATM to get some money." John Barley Corn had identification on him, so I thought, "What the hell, it will be an easy ride."

John Barley Corn: I have to go by Western Union to pick up some money.

Patty: John was directing me to go all over back streets in North Las Vegas. I was scared, I radio in, and told dispatch exactly where I was at every turn. I did not realize that John was drunk. Mr. Barley Corn got his money, and paid me. He wanted me me to take him some where else.

Patty: John, your ride with me is over.

One of my friends picked up customer downtown, and the customer stabbed Jay in the neck. Killings, and stabbing make me nervous.

Hound Dawg posted this message in July on his web site.

At about 11P.M, on Thursday night, an unnamed driver picked up a fare at Jerry's Nugget Casino. The second such incident was from the same casino in thirty hours. The driver was taken to 1915 Simmons, where he reportedly hit the driver over the head with a rock, and took his money. The suspect was described as a black male, five feet to six feet, one hundred and forty pounds. He was wearing a t-shirt, and blue pants.

Patty: When Tu Pac Shaiur was killed in Las Vegas, he was in a car on Flamingo Road. From what I understand, he had a fight with Mr. Big at the MGM Hotel. The doorman told me that Tu Pad Shaiur had kicked Mr. Big. The police closed down Flamingo road, since Las Vegas police pride themselves on being able to protect it's visitors, the Vegas police were in rage.

6

There was a killing in Laughlin, Nevada. Forty thousand motorcyclists go for their annual river run once a year, The Hell's Angels, and the Mongols were not getting on with each other. It makes perfect sense to me that craze motorcyclists started killing people in Harrah's Hotel. Three people were killed, and a dozen were wounded. Believe me, they are not like Marlon Brando in the, "The Wild One."

I remember seeing all of the Hell's Angels in San Francisco, they always look like they needed a bath to me.

It use to be safe in Las Vegas for a taxicab driver to drive at night time, but as Mark told me, "at night, they are animals."

At the Paris Hotel, some person stole a car then crashed, and jumped into a taxicab.

CHAPTER TEN
HATRED OF FOREIGN TAXICAB DRIVERS

There is a real hatred among cab drivers over Muslims and all of the other foreigners in Las Vegas. I am all for capitalism, but these people are taking over our jobs.

Okeyl Dokey posted this message in April.

Talking about stories, you hear from customers, about how one of the taxicab drivers, (invariably Arab, throws a fit, and scares the customer into giving him a bigger tip. I have heard that one so many times, that I have the routine down pat.

Ariel Sharon posted this message in April on VC.

So, that's what they are. You are describing these types with a lot of mannerisms, the Arabs, and Muslims, all middle easterners for that fact (sic), are ninety percent of all the problems we deal with daily. They are not only the most dishonest taxicab drivers but also the most reckless, rude, inconsiderate drivers in Las Vegas.

7

One would hope that the Taxicab Authority would fully investigate these people before we issue them taxicab licenses. These people are the best-documented foreigners know to humanity. I find it hard to believe that they are legal. You can see them in their groups, talking in a language that only they can understand.

Patty: I do not blame our immigrants for talking with people who share their language. It is very difficult to learn a new language. Americans are not linguists, when I was in Napel, I practically pounced on a man who could speak English.

Ariel: You always see them hugging each other, shaking hands or fondling each other somehow, and you never hear them talk about any women. Are they all faggots?

Patty: When I was in the Middle East, all the men that I was dating were certainly not faggots. Maybe, we can get Ariel to become our next Ambassador to the United Nations.

This message was posted by Nippy in May on www.vegascabbie.com

The Paris Hotel used to be a good cab stand until certain Eastern Europeans (Bosnians and Russians ruined it.

Patty: There are not any Russians at the Paris, just people from Yugoslavia, I called them the Yugoslavian Mafia.

Nippy: They get out of their cabs talk to each other and will leave empty gaps (three cabs lengths long.) form in a line. They tighten the line, and will not move their cabs until they are finished talking to each other.

Meanwhile, other drivers cannot fit onto the end of the cab line or they would be stuck in the tunnel until these guys would finished talking They wrote anti-American slogans on the wall, and things like, "Europeans Only." They try to keep other drivers out of the Paris in an attempted ammo-like take over of the stand.

Patty: I asked one of the doormen, if the Yugoslavians wrote on the wall of the tunnel about their hatred of Americans. Joe told me, "No."

Patty: They are not that dumb.

The tunnel was similar to Bellagio's, and had a bathroom, and coffee for the cab drivers. Once, I was at the Paris Hotel, and I turned down near Las Vegas Blvd to get back into line; the cab driver told me "I was staging at the wrong area." I told the Serb, "I was in the right place." He told one of his Serb friends to block me, and then the driver took my place.

This message was posted on VC in August by Limo Driver.

The state of Florida has changed its opinion and is letting Muslims women cab drivers have their picture on their driver's license with their face covered.

Patty: I cannot believe that any responsible taxicab authority would do this. All thieves in Miami are putting on their veil so the cops will not be able to recognize them.

We have a supervisor that said some derogatory remarks to one of the immigrants. The man was threatening Jose if he did not shape up, he would send him home and he wouldn't be able to drive. I came down on the supervisor and told him to never talk to Jose like that again. The immigrants have enough problems with out having to deal with some seven dollars a hour supervisor.

CHAPTER ELEVEN
PETTY AND JUVENILE DRIVERS

Hound Dawg posted this message in April on his own site.

I guess I haven't paid enough attention, but it has bought to my attention through our message board that trash cans at the airport have been removed from the taxi staging area up by the booth. At a recent PDA meeting, I discovered the reason was that several drivers set fire to a couple of cans to protest tickets that were given out to a driver. Apparently, the taxicab authority police officer was screwing up, at always.

It brings me to the question, why again are the majority of drivers being punished for the actions of an ignorant few? I am in full agreement that those starting the fire should be held fully accountable for their actions. Removal of the cans is only going to present a bigger problem, I am afraid. Please consider this.

Patty: Any visitors who come to Las Vegas via air has to pay an airport tax for the privilege of visiting "Happy Land." Cab drivers have to buy some tickets that cost one dollar, and twenty cents. As we go through the booth, the airport police takes the ticket. The driver goes over spikes that counts how many people have come to Las Vegas. God, forbid, if the airport police do not have the count right.

Patty: At the booth, the airport has put up three or four trash cans. When the drivers are coming up the line, the cab driver would get rid of their trash. They would try to be "Babe Ruth," and it ended up that the trash was missing the cans. Therefore, the airport police removed the trash cans from the booth, and put them down in the pit. You can see that this is one of the most important policies to the drivers life since the end of World War Two, What did the taxi cab driver think would happen, if they were so slovenly too miss the damn trash cans?

This message was posted in April on www.vegascabbie.com

Well, can anyone tell me if there are any trashcans up near the booth at the airport? HELL ,NO, we cannot even get a trash cans where we want them. I say, "Let's throw trash there anyway."

Patty: Most of the drivers seem to be doing this anyway.

Driver: In addition, make them clean it up, and I do not just mean bottles, and cans. Let's throw some food out there, which will attract some nice RED ants, that will bite their asses when they sit on the stool in the booth. I bet someone will put some trash cans up there.

CHAPTER TWELVE
TREACHERY IN THE TAXI CAB BUSINESS IN LAS VEGAS, OR BECOME A SUPERVISOR, AND GET FIRED.

10

When Jack was fired for taking bribes at YCS, we all thought that he had been sat up, (which he was.) and in unionism, we felt very bad for him. I felt like I had lost my personal helper. I was one of the people who went to talk to Bill Shranko about hiring Jack back.

Bill: There isn't any way that Jack can come back to YCS. I miss Jack too, but he shouldn't have taken the money.

Patty: Bill could have warned Jack because Bill had a late phone call, I assume, from Pete. I would have called Jack and told him to come in and be "clean." After all, Jack had been there for ten years. When Bill Shranko took over the supervisor job at YCS, he put in a new rule that cab drivers could not tip anyone, and we would be fired if we gave gratuities.

Management at YCS gave this driver five hundred dollars to set up Jack., She gave Jack one hundred dollars and kept four hundred for herself. Was she a typical taxicab driver, I think not.

At Christmas time, I went over to see Jack at Union Cab. I felt so bad for Jack that I followed him to Charlie Frias Company. With-in a year, he was made general manager. What does he do? He get involved with taking bribes. One of the drivers told me, "Jack was taking one hundred dollars from driver, if they wanted to take a week off."

I told Jack on different occasions that he was being watched and he told me, "better people have tried to catch me." A driver came in an asked Jack for the twelve to twelve shift and Jack told him,"it will cost you one thousand dollars. The driver went and told Charlie, and Jack and his faithful secretary, Gen were both fired.

If, I had known that I could have gotten off the 6 or 7 A.M shift to the 7:30 shift,. I would have gladly paid the thousand dollars. Maybe, Jack was becoming to greedy to put it mildly! My friends at YCS told me not to go over to Frias, because Charlie likes to fire people.

A taxicab driver from YCS told me that he was glad that I was writing my book. Dear Owners of the taxicab business, "you would be surprised, when I tell you, how many people have told me, "I was right."

When I went to Friars, Jack told me,"it is alright to tip the supervisors." I could not tip enough, twenties, and forty dollars were flying out of my purse. I am so insecure that people might feel that I am cheap that I over compensate on how much money to tip.

If I wanted to take a day off, I would give twenty dollars to my supervisor. If a supervisor is particularity greedy, he will take money from everyone. All Charlie has to do is look out his window and see all of the cabs that are there. The supervisor will be fired. I asked one of my bosses how I could get away with coming back to work early. He told me, "they always covered for me."

We bid for out shifts at the cab companies in order of seniority. When I missed my bid at Union Cab, I was so upset that I told my supervisor that I wanted to go home, " He told me, "You can't go home because I need you to drive." I tried to bribe him with a twenty dollars bill. He took the money, put it in his pocket, and still said "no" to me. I thought this was so fumy. I was lucky to even get a shift, I had to get up so early that my cats did not wake up.

And, so it goes.

Season's Greetings

Happy Holidays
from the Bellagio
day shift Doorman

Buddy,
    Ron &
        Steve

CHAPTER THIRTEEN
HOTEL AND CASINO OWNERS

The Alladin Hotel is in bankruptcy. The original person, Mr. Sumner, who put up the money had been through bankruptcies in New York City, and Brooklyn. How. Mr. Sumner though he was going to come to Las Vegas and make money is beyond me. Mr. Sumner was not all that swift and Mom controlled the money.

Four days before the Alladin Hotel was to open, Mr. Sumner sent written invitations to all of the drivers to come over and learn how to pick up and drop off, he also promised us a lunch or a dinner made by one of his famous chefs. (MacDonald's)

Dear Readers: Do you know what Mr. Sumner gave us? A cheese sandwich and some Oreo cookies.

I do not pretend to be an astute business person, but why would a person want to alienate all of the taxicab drivers in Las Vegas? If the hotel gives an opening date, the hotel has to make it and Mr. Sumner did not get a fire permit! All of his customers' were going to Motel Six!

Mr. Sumner could not pay his bills and Mom would not give him anymore bread. There is a saying in Las Vegas, "An outsider comes to town with money, and leaves Las Vegas without dime."

ANGER. There is still a lot of anger from the taxicab drivers about the doormen putting "Big Spenders," in Limousines. I e-mailed Jim Talley about how the doormen get away with their, "Limousine number?" Do they whisper to the customers?"

Jim: What I have seen happen many times is a bunch of guys walk onto the line and talk to the doorman. They talk for just a short time, and then they re escorted off to the side Along comes the Limo, and they are off. Cabs and doormen generally are not in hearing distance, no whispering required

Patty: It is written in fire that you are not suppose to tip a doorman for a long ride. I would personally tip the doorman, and I must say that I get along with the doormen so well, they have always refused any money from me. I feel that the limousines are the property of the hotels, and they can damn well do what they want to do with the Limos. Taxicab drivers do not seem to understand that we are only one step above bus drivers.

The next message was posted by GTA in reference to the complaints about the Doormen.

What do you mean? We are paid good money for doing Jack shit! If it were not for the doormen and their generally good skills, the majority of you dumb drivers would bring chaos to these hotels, making the customers angry at the city and us. Tens of thousands of people were laid off in this town after September 11th and yet all the doormen still have jobs. Something ponder.

Patty: Amen.

Patty: The drivers are also angry about the doormen putting in only one customer in their cabs during conventions. I asked Steve about the drivers complaint:

Steve: Bellagio's arranges to have buses take their customers to conventions. Most people do not want to ride with people, they do not know.

Patty: After all, politicians do not want to divulge any state secrets like how we are going to get out of Iraq.

I do not like the doorman at the Rio Hotel because he cheated me out of fifty dollars. I asked him "if he would change a one hundred dollars for me, which he did by giving me a lot of fives, and one dollar bills." He got rid of me fast, and it was only later, that I realize I was missing fifty dollars One of the drivers told me that "I should have gone back to the doorman and confronted him." but, when someone steals from you, they would just act indigent, saying "How could you think I would do something like that to you?"

Patty: Easy man. I have seen you give airport rides to your friends. I said nothing to him.

At Bellagios' one day, someone left a five dollar bill in the back seat of my car. Steve, the doorman noticed the five, and " he told me to pick it up."

Steve never reveals his moods. I am just like James, and when it is slow, James get angry and depressed, especially if he is not being tipped. James told me,"he had been stiffed twenty-two times in a row." John from the MGM told me, "that his all time record was thirty-six times."

At the Las Vegas Hilton, a doorman has been there for a hundred years, he is so gruff that everyone was afraid of him, So, when I go to the Las Vegas Hilton, I have started calling him, "my sweets." Guess what readers? It worked, and he is always very nice to me.

Michael Squires of the Las Vegas Journal apparently had written an article about the dishonesty of Las Vegas taxi drivers. How dare he? This was my response to all of the complaints on www. vegascabbie.com.

Patty: I do not see why all of you drivers are surprised that we are called thieves. We are suffering under a collection of guilt. How many times have you heard stories about the twenty-five dollar charges from the airport to Bellagios?

I have done a lot of traveling, and my perception of taxicab drivers in Las Vegas has changed. Our international cab drivers do not like us, and they will do anything to make a dollar, because they are sending money back home.

The other side:Most of the taxicab drivers that I know were basically honest. They know the ropes, and just went so far. Mark was incredibly honest, he should be head of the Federal Reserve.

JUST FOR THE FUN OF IT.

My friend, Suzi Q, and I decided to evaluate the differences between being a taxicab driver or a doorman.

TAXI CAB PROS: They can sit in an air-condition car all day long. The can eat and call people on their cell phones. At the airport, they can play cards or run around and talk to each other, or court their next girl friend.

CON: They do not make very much money.

DOORMEN PRO: They make a lot of money.

CON: They have to stand for eight hours in the cold and hot weather, and it is killing during the summer time. They have to open doors and load luggage, and be stiffed by rude people.

Patty: From a monetary point of view, I will swing with the doormen. It just isn't for the money, they are all so bright and funny and I like smart people. All of the doormen have to go to "stress classes and learn to hold their tempers.

One of the complaints that the drivers have made is "doormen are over paid." Quote: You can train a "monkey to grab luggage and put it where it is suppose to be. Another complaint was with the MGM doormen wearing monkey uniforms.

Patty: My response to all of this bullshit. I have never had one problem with the doormen at the MGM. Furthermore, how many times have you heard a taxicab driver yell, "Fuck You," to a doorman. Believe me, this does not win any accolades from the Doors. As far as their outfits go, I just love the scummer taxicab drivers who have not taken a bath in six months, wear clothes that belong to Mosses, and their breath smells like a ash can.

Steve Wynn has built the La Reeve Hotel for one billion, eighty three million dollars. The hotel has an eight story mountain and an enclosing three-acre lake in front of the property. It has been Mr.

Wynn, imagination who has created modern Las Vegas. He built Bellagio's, Mirage, and the Treasure island. 'Goody, goody for us.

I have just read a book about Steve Wynn, in it the author stated that Mr. Wynn consorted with gangsters. It is the most ridiculous book I have ever read. When Mr. Wynn came to Las Vegas, gangsters owned all of the hotels. From what I understand, Mr. Wynn sued the author and came away with one-half million dollars. I have always felt that any criticism of Mr. Wynn was fueled by jealously.

When Mr. Wynn built Bellagio's, he took the cream of the crop of his employees from his other hotels that he owned to Bellagio's. Steve was one of the doorman at Bellagio's, and he had worked as a bellman at the Mirage Hotel for a number of years. He also worked on the side door at the Mirage for around five or six years. Buddy, Thomas, and Ron all worked at the Treasure Island as doormen, Steve is always teasing Ron about taking his job at the T.I.

Steve is as cool as the "other side of a pillow." I was driving into Bellagio's, and I almost hit him, he just raised his eyebrows. What fun I had with all of the doormen, besides trying to kill one of them.

Mr Wynn sold all of his hotels to Kirk Kerekorian, and when he bought the Desert Inn, he converted it into La Reeve Hotel, he did not have a place to send his help while the hotel was being built. Mr. Wynn has said, "This was the worse experience of my life." (Not a bad guy.)

When Steve Wynn bought the Desert Inn, he had been trying to buy all of the homes on the D.I. I picked up a gentleman from Iran, who wanted to go to his home on the Desert Inn. He told me, "Mr. Wynn offered him two and a half million dollars for his home, but he was holding out for five million dollars. He also told Mr. Wynn, "if I do not get this amount, I might open a strip club or a gas station on my property. I saw his home and if he could get seventy-fifty thousand dollars for it, he would be lucky

John, from the MGM, had worked under the mob, he told me, "The help was treated much better, because the house made enough money in other parts of the Casino's. When the corporations came in, they decided that they wanted every part of the hotel to make money."

Patty: I think that I would rather have preferred working for the mob instead of Weight Watchers Corporation. After all, what do the COS know about gambling, and killing.

Brian, one of the doormen at the MGM went on vacation, and while he was gone, Patrick worked part of his shift. I asked Patrick,"Where is Brian?"

Patrick: He is marching in a gay parade in San Francisco.

Patty: (From Seinfeld, not that there is anything wrong with be gay.) I thought,"what difference does it make, I am from San Francisco, where anything goes." I told my girlfriend Susie Q. and she could not believe it. When Brian came back from his vacation, "I asked him how he liked San Francisco?"

Brian: I went to Laguna Beach, California.

Patty: I thought to myself, "Well, Laguna Beach has a large gay population.

Brian: I am not gay. I have a wife and two kids. How many people did Patrick tell this lie too."

Patty: Everyone.

I never knew that Patrick had such a great sense of humor. I will kill Patrick.

At Bellagio's, one of the taxicabs caught on fire in the tunnel. It was an electrical fire,and everyone had to get out of the tunnel fast. I was driving into Bellagio's to pick up and the head of security started yelling at me to "get out." He wanted me to turn around and leave by the other driveway, where other customers' were driving in, I knew if that I went that way, I would hit a car. He was still yelling and screaming at me when I told him, "I will hit a car." He kept on screaming at me, so I just said to him, "GO FUCK YOURSELF."

One of the security guards ran up to me and told me, "If I ever talked that way again, they were going to call my supervisor."

Patty: Go ahead, I am not use to someone yelling and screaming at me. I was beginning to sound like a truck driver and the security guard was talking to me like I was a taxicab driver.

I was at the New York, New York Two, and I was leaving which means I was going around the back of the hotel, and there was some building construction going on. There was a taxicab in front of me, and two big trucks in the lead. A woman construction lady was standing with her big sign which said, GO SLOW or STOP. It was taking a long time for the trucks to move. The taxicab driver decided to just move around the truck to get out. The woman was waving her sign that said, "STOP, and she was screaming at the driver as if her, STOP AND GO sign was made in stone. I could not stop laughing, my sick sense of humor.

I went to the Sahara Hotel, and one of the doormen made fun of the way I spoke.

Patty: I have a speech problem.

Doorman: I am really sorry.

Patty: It's alright because I have had to deal with this problem for years and years."

I was at the MGM the other day, and I asked John how some customer's beat him?.

John: Customer's toss chips at you from the El Rancho Hotel which has been closed for years, also they run the "give me twenty dollars and then ask for five dollars back routine."

One of the taxicab drivers said, "the name of the Venetian Hotel is so stupid that I won't pick up there."

Patty: I do not know where this taxicab driver is from, probably from, "Friends Wood, Texas," but the Venetian Hotel is so beautiful that it takes my breath away. The venetian has canals running through the hotel and you can ride on a gondolier. (Don't forget to tip.) The Venetian is so spectacular that when I am bringing customers for their first visit, I always bring my fares to the front door, because if you look up and, you are greeted with Michaelangelo's paintings. Another complaint from one of the drivers was " Mr.Sheldon put in speed bumps coming through the back of the hotel."

Patty: Mr. Sheldon did this because the drivers were speeding.

Authority on Hotels Taxi Driver: Mr. Sheldon stiffed many contractors, forcing some builders into bankruptcy.

Patty: Mr. Sheldon has been living in Las Vegas for years, now why would he ruined his reputation by not paying his contractor's? If you work for him, you had better do work up to his expeditions, or he will raise hell, as he should.

Another complaint from the drivers is that the rides from the Venetian only go to the Mirage, Treasure Island, and Bellagio's.

Patty: In the first place, when you have a short ride to the Mirage Hotel or to Caesar's, the doorman always tells you to come back to the front of the line and they will give you another ride. Of course, if you have not been polite to the door and scream about the short ride, I do not think that doorman will have much empathy for you. I would like to take people to Bellagio's Hotel or to the Venetian Hotel all day long. These customers have cash and they are always willing to part with some of their money.

I was thrown off the Venetian Hotel property today. Security was checking cars going in, and letting the taxicab waltz right into the drop off. The Venetian started to do this right after September 11th. A few months later, the Venetian began checking the taxicabs too.

Patty: I drove right by security and this guy came running up to my car and told me to STOP.

Michael: I want to check your car.

Patty: Well, you must have changed the rules, because I have always gone right through the line.

Michael: No Taxicabs have gone by me.

Patty: From my lips, came one of my derogatory remarks.

Michael: No one is going to talk to me that way. You can not come on the Venetian property today.

Patty: I thought to myself, I do not mind if I was 86th off of the Imperial Palace, but not the Venetian Hotel. I immediately turned around and went back to talk to Michael.

Patty: I am sorry, and I lied to Michael and told him " a customer had beat me today and I was not my self. Please let me back on the Venetian. Michael, you should not have to stand for my language, or anyone's bad language. Michael is a good guy and he always is laughing when he sees me.

I go to the MGM in the morning because it is a good short ride. I go to the Venetian in the after noon. But, my heart belongs to Bellagios. Once, I had not been to Bellagio's for a few days. Steve asked me "what is wrong Patty? Don't you play Bellagio's anymore?

Patty: I had a breakdown with my car.

Steve: I have breakdowns too, but I always make it too work.

I was down in the garage at Bellagio's where the taxicab drivers line up to pick up. There were two guys sitting at a a table, provided by Bellagio's, in case the drivers want to eat, the drivers had about thirty watches on the table to sell to the other drivers. Sound's like Capitalism at it's best.

I was at Bellagio's Hotel, and when I first started driving, I picked up a fare, and as I was moving out, I started to write on my trip sheet. Steve just look at me, put his fingers to his lips and said, "No." I would like to say that I learned to drive a cab because of the doormen, but I decided that this would not be an complement to the Doors because of my driving.

CHAPTER FOURTEEN
CUSTOMERS LIKE YOU MAKE ME WANT TO GO BACK TO BEING A HOOKER

Because I was not allowed to swear at my customers, I felt that it was necessary for me to come up with something that I considered insulting, and that Dear Reader's is how I came up with, "Customer's Like You Make Me Want to Go Back To Being a Hooker. "

Well, I got beat today, this is the first time for me. I picked up Dillinger at the Mandalay Bay Hotel, he wanted to go to the Monte Carlo Hotel. Dillinger was a nice clean looking man. (All that glitters is not gold.)

On the way over to the hotel, Dillinger asked me if " I could change a one hundred dollar bill for him." No, I replied. When we reached the hotel, he told me that he would have to go into the hotel to get his money changed. I asked him for his wallet and he said, "no." He promised me that he would be right back.

Naturally, he did not come back to my car, the tab was eight dollars. I went around to the "pick up," and told the doorman what happened to me. I asked my next customer's, "If they would mind if I did not put the meter on to the airport?" I told them "I would charge you eight dollars." My fares told me, "We understand and it is all right with us." I have aways been some-what shy to tell people to leave their wallet or their luggage in my car while they are changing their money, but not now., I walk in with Rhett to get their money exchanged.

I was was at Bellagio's and I was saying good-by to Steve, and this customer said to me, "I do not want to pay for your conversation with the doorman." I told him that I would give him the nickel that it cost him for me to talk to Steve.

Carl started yelling at me to "get going." Take off any money that you have put on the meter where it evolves you, and the doorman. On the way out, I felt that I was not in the mood for this fare. For the first time I said "Customers Like You Make Me Want To Go Back To Being A Hooker." (Saying that phrase felt so good.) "Just get out my cab," which he did and he started walking up the hill to Bellagio's. I just hope that the next cab driver did not try talk with one of the Doors.

Dear Reader's, do you feel that maybe I do not have the temperament to drive a cab? Steve and the other doormen would never let their emotions get in their way of doing a good job. Maybe, I should take one of doormen anger classes!

On Sunday, I went to work at four o'clock in the morning, and I picked up my first fares at the MGM Hotel. Three girls were going to the Stardust Hotel, the first thing they say to me, "Don't take us the wrong way." The Stardust Hotel is right down Las Vegas Blvd. I said to the girls,"Please do not start this one with me. Let me give you some advice, when we get to your destination and if you feel you have been long hauled, get out of my cab and refuse to pay the fare."

They agreed with me and I told the girls the name of my book and they promised to buy it. Always promoting.

I was at the airport, and party of nine had to split into two cabs. One of the girls climbed into my front seat, and threw everything on the floor. She asked me,"How much does it cost to go to Bellagio's?"

Patty: If you are going to Bellagio's, you should not be asking me how much it will costs. It costs (anywhere from nine to twelve dollars depending on the traffic.) She then started to tell me how to drive. Finally, I said to her, " you have taken over everything in this cab, just relax, and I will get you to Bellagio's." It was their first time to Las Vegas, and I told them that,you are living on "High cotton."

I had the fucking Russians, who lived in San Francisco, Mr and Mrs. Stalin were going to the Bellagio's. Dear Readers, I have told you that it was foreigners who were rude and condescending. Both of the Stalin's treated me as if I was a barbarian in Russia.

I picked up two women from the Venetian and I was taking them to the MGM. Since the strip was so busy, I told them I was going the back way over Kovel.

Cheap Lady: I want to buy some cigarettes.

Patty: Why don't you 't buy the cigarettes at the hotel?

Cheap Lady: Because I do not want to pay eight dollars a pack."

Patty: That seems like a good idea to me.

Cheap Lady: Is that the MGM hotel to the right?

Patty: I am taking you around the back, where there is an entrance to the MGM to save time, You do not think that I am trying to pad your bill, do you?

Cheap Lady: I know exactly what the ride is cost."

Patty: The bill was six dollars and ten cents. When we arrived at the MGM hotel, she paid me even money. I said to Cheap Lady, "Customers Like You Make Me Want to Go Back to Being a Hooker." Get out of my cab and do not come back to Las Vegas."

You might think that this is going to far, but, you have to understand, that I do not long haul people, at least not to the MGM.

I picked up a gentleman at the MGM, and I told him about "Cheap Lady. " George worked at the MGM "welcoming desk,." He told me that " people are screaming all day long, he wished that he could say to people,"Customer's Like You Make Me Want To Go Back To Being a Hooker."

Customer's are always trying to have their bills reduced. They complain that the water does not come out of the faucets fast enough; that their neighbors in the hotel are too loud. These people are in Las Vegas, not Chillicothe, Ohio.

A few months ago, the electricity in the hotel went down for half an hour. Customer's were coming to George and "telling him that they were scared, and asked him to deduct fifty dollars off their bill." The MGM graciously took the money off of their bill.

When customer's make their reservations at any hotel on the strip, they always ask for a room facing Las Vegas Blvd. The hotel takes their requests but they cannot promise a room that overlooks Las Vegas Blvd, unless of course, you are George Clooney. Sometimes, Bill Blow becomes so enraged when he does not get the room overlooking Las Vegas,Blvd, he starts yelling at George.

People from Asia are terrible tips. In fact, the Americans are the best tips, just like my English customers told me.

I picked up this gentleman at about four-thirty in the afternoon, he wanted to go out to Summerlin which is long ride. I started to go on the freeway and he told me that he didn't want to go that way. "Fine, I replied." He wanted to go over Jones," I told my master that "I would take him anyway that he wanted go." Mr. Fay also told me that the ride only costs thirty five dollars when he went from his home to the airport early Sunday morning. Going on Jones in the middle of day, when it is busy costs a lot more money.

I had just started driving. I told this Sadistic rat, "I would turn off the meter at the thirty five dollar point." What a fool I was to let this bastard intimidate me. Jones was very busy and he told me to drive faster. At thirty fine dollars, I turned off the meter. I beat my self out of ten dollars.

I picked up three people who were from Vancouver, Canada. On the way to Mandalay Bay, I asked the girl,"if foreigners were taking over the taxi cab business in Canada?" She told me,"they are all over the place and you could not find a Canadian who was driving a cab." I replied, "I do not like to see Americans being pushed out of a profession.

Bad Canadian:The jobs are not our jobs

Patty: That is fine and dandy, but foreigners will work for nothing and will never organize and this is not the American way. At least, in every other state except Nevada.

Bad Canadian: You had better change your attitude.

I picked up two Mexicans who wanted to go the Bank of America, I suggested a B/A that was closer and Jose started yelling at me. I picked up my little note book to write down this experience. One of the customer's saw me writing and Domingo started being nice to me. I told,"Jose and Domingo, never yell at Las Vegas Taxicab drivers, because we are not like taxicab drivers in Mexico City."

If you want to live on the edge, take a ride with a Mexican cab driver, no meters in the car, and you usually have to bargain over the fare. If you have a car, you had better ask the Mexican gentleman to watch your car, if you do not, they might just steal your car. I understand that it is very dangerous walking around Mexico City, but I just love this city, I remember dancing all night long, and I do not dance!

I was in Cairo, Egypt, and I was with,"my love of the night, he showed me all of the parts that had been stolen from his Porsche.

I picked up two girls at the Hilton which is at the end of the strip, and they wanted to go to Mandalay Bay Hotel. On the way over, they were telling me how terrible, and what a bad experience they had at Mandalay Hotel. The food wasn't any good, the pool area is terrible and that no one is nice and friendly. Their predicament surprised me, because I have always heard good things about the Manadaly Bay Hotel.

I was driving the girls the back way, and her bill was going up to nine dollars. She said to me, "the the ride should only cost eight dollars."There isn't anyway that the trip from the Hilton to Mandalay could cost eight dollars. As a matter of fact, the ride should cost fifteen dollars.

I decided that these two, sweet girls, were completely wrong about the Mandalay Bay Hotel. The hotel has the a beautiful pool area, The food is good and they have wonderful doormen.

I picked up a couple at the Mandalay and they were going to the Venetian. Paul Getty told me, "employees of hotels should not be tipped for services rendered." Paul told me that he would not tip maids. I told him that most of the maids are from Latin America and they do not make that much money. (Let's hope that customers take care of the maids.) NOW GET THIS ONE; Mrs, Getty told me,"it cost less to live in Mexico, so they should be grateful for the money that they earned here.

Patty: What does that have to with anything? The Latin Americans live in Las Vegas now and the cost of living in much higher. I could not believe that anyone could be that stupid.

Paul: I do not like to tip the doorman.

Patty: You should tip the Doors or they might drop your luggage on your head. I could hardly wait to get this couple out of my car.

I picked up a Japanese man, and his family at the airport. He could not speak very good English. He wanted to go to the Rivera Hotel, which is at the end of the strip.

Tojo: I want to go down Paradise and do not take the freeway.

Patty: I am going down Paradise.

Tojo: I am the boss and you are the driver.

Patty: After the third time of this, "I am the boss number." I finally said to him: "Who in the hell do you think you are talking too?"

Tojo: I am the boss.

Patty: Tojo reached over and hit me on my arm. I was so angry with him that I started screaming, we won the war, not you. I would have called the Taxi Cab Authority, but it would have taken over an hour for the TA to get to me, and I was making money. When we arrived at the Riviera Hotel, I told the doorman that this bastard had hit me, the Door had people to load into my cab, and he looked bored with this whole episode.

I picked up a customer at the Paris Hotel, who was from Hawaii, and was rolling into Las Vegas to see the Three Tenors. He was so condescending too me abut going to see, "The Three Tenors," that I decided that this taxicab driver was going to see Carreras, Domingo, and Pavarotti. Actually, I had been vacillating about seeing the three of them for a month. I went home, got out my credit card, called Mandalay Hotel, and asked them how much a ticket would cost me? The lowest price was six hundred dollars. Since I am hard of hearing, I like to sit close to the stage, I asked them what the next price was and the ticket seller said nine hundred dollars. I told the ticket agent that "I would go for the nine hundred dollars."

Dear Readers: Do you know I was looking for this gentleman from Hawaii. I was hoping that I was in front of him, or better yet, sitting right next to me.

It was the first time that I had ever gone to a concert where you can see the singers better on the the television screen that you can on stage. I felt that I should have been on the theater platform sitting on their lap for what I paid. Never again, will I go to a large room to hear a singer. I felt like I was at a Madonna concert.

I talked to some people who were coming from the airport and I told them how much I paid for ticket to see the "Three Tenors." My customer told me that he loses thousands of dollars at the casinos, so who is the smart one?

I was driving down Las Vegas Blvd with some Mexicans, and we had to stop at Tropicana Blvd. Susie Q. was right next to me in her cab, I kept trying to catch her attention, but she was telling her customer's, "stories and lies." Understand, the light was still red, and Jose told me, "concentrate on your driving." When I told Susie Q, she said to me, "Why didn't you tell him to, "go to hell." I must admit that sometimes, I am so taken a back by bad manners, that I do not say anything.

I picked up at the Venetian, a gentleman, his wife and whose son lived in Las Vegas. They were going to New York, New York Too.

When we stopped from traffic, this is what he said to me.

Bad Passenger: The meter keeps on running?

Patty: That's right sir.

Bad passenger: Turn off the meter.

Patty: I cannot sir, it is against rule number five thousand and five.

Bad Passenger: Turn off the meter. I think that you are thief. Do you hear me, turn off the meter!

Patty: Would you like to get out?

Bad Passenger: Yes, I would..

Patty: I stopped at Bellagio's driveway and let him out of my car. In retrospect, why didn't his dumb son say anything. He lived in Las Vegas, but I felt that probably,"Jumbo Dumbo," had never ridden in a cab before.

I picked up a guy that kept telling me that Joe Montana was a jerk. We were on the freeway, and I thought to myself, if I throw him out of the cab right now, I may just lose my job. If I was in San Francisco, the cab company would probably give me a star.

CHAPTER FIFTEEN
ACCIDENTS, FACTS OF LIFE, AND MY SPELLING

When we hit someone we are suppose to stop immediately and make no moves. The cab accident supervisor comes out to the scene of the crime, takes pictures and determines who was at fault. I hit a car at the Convention Center, the Desert cab driver was smart or more experience then me and he had a witness sign a form saying that it was my fault for rolling back on the cab. (Believe me, it was my fault.) I just lied, and said it was his fault. I was so stupid, there wasn't any damage to either one of our cars. We could have gone right back to work, and no one would have known the better.

At this time, I would like to say, Desert Cab, where ever you are, I am sorry that I insisted on calling in the accident.

I was at the airport pit, I opened the driver's side door, and my car was hit by another cab. The driver was coming up the lane too fast and he practically took off my left hand door. The cabbie was from a third world country and all of his friends were saying that " it was my fault," The American driver started sticking up for me. With world war three in the spotlight, my supervisor told me that he was "hep" to what was happening and he called it a 50-50 accident.

I now had two accidents and on the third accident, I would be fired. (Three strikes and you are out.) I was making a left turn to go into the MGM, and another women was making a right turn. We hit each other and I took off her driver's side window, and scraped her door. I do not know if the accident was my fault, or her fault. I told her to find out how much it would cost to have the car fixed, and I would pay her. With-in a few days, she called me and told me that it would cost seven hundred and fifty dollars. I met her outside of Sam's Casino, gave her the money, and she walked into Sam's to gamble.

I was at the Paris Hotel, and I was always hitting the statues outside of the hotel. I was destroying my right hand mirror. The doormen told me to say that it was windy and that the wind blew off my mirror. Another time, I hit the statue, so, when I went into work, I told the mechanics that some guy, "was riding a bike down Las Vegas Blvd and hit my mirror."

I was on the way to the convention center, and I tapped this taxicab driver on his fender. He jumped out, and told me that he had to call the Taxicab Authority. I could have killed this guy, he kept on telling me that it was part of the procedure.

My immediate supervisor said to me, "what am I going to with you?" I replied to him, "Why don't you fire me?" Now here is the guy that I have been showering with ten and twenty dollar bills. (I know that I am repeating myself.) " What is he going to do with me?" I should have said, "Go down to the bank."

I was in the line at the Mandalay Bay Hotel, I saw a driver who worked for Lucky Cab. I asked the driver to "please, find Jo Jo the Greek for me," My car started rolling, I hit the taxicab in front of me, the cabbie was reading a book and he nearly jumped out of his skin. I told the driver that I would be in trouble if they called in on me. He looked at the other driver and told him,"nothing happen here," or something to that affect. Jo Jo called me that night, and "I told him that, "I would never make it as a taxicab driver, he just laughed and told me not to worry."

At Yellow cab at three o'clock in the morning, I kept hitting the back end of driver who was in front of me in the parking lot. Finally, the driver left a note for me saying " if you do not stop, and desist hitting me, I will call the authorities on you. I know who you are." The only thing, I can say in my self defense is that it is very dark in the early winter's morning.

I was at the airport, and all drivers had been told which lane is for certain traffic. Naturally, I went down the wrong lane, one of the airport police ran up to me screaming, you are in the wrong lane."

When Rick realized that it was me, He said, "Oh, it is you, Patty, and with that, he told me where to go and he did not give me a ticket.

So, be it.

If you want to hear about all of the accidents, please click on to <u>www.accidentspatty.com</u>

FACTS OF LIFE.

A customer told me that he was not used too senior citizens driving a cab. This really hurt my feelings. So, I had a face lift, and laser treatments, the doctor told me, "it would take me about a month to recover." It took three months before I could stop wearing a scarf around my face. This was rather embarrassing to me. I talked to the doctor and he told me, " I must have gone too far into your face." It would seem to me that a doctor should know all of the medical problems that could arise to a patient while he is whirling his scalper. He told me to come back into the office and he would do the rest of my face for nothing. I decided to pass on the doctor. If you work for the public, you want to look as wonderful as you can for, "Mr. Tipper."

Since, I have had my face lift, an Ethiopian driver has tried to pull up my dress.

A customer wanted to massage my neck. A taxicab driver wanted to come over to my apartment and,"visit with me." I asked the driver if he was married and he told me, " yes." I told him to"get out of my cab."

When a doorman told me that I looked beautiful, I did not care whether he was married or not. The most wonderful complement, I received was from Patrick, the doorman at the MGM, "How old are you, about forty or forty two?"

I do not mind dying, it's the deterioration of the body that I hate. I wish that we all were in good health until we reached ninety years old, and we could just die in our sleep. I just want to go to the,"Big Bartender." in the sky gracefully.

I had a stroke in San Francisco and lost my voice, it was depressing to say the least. When doctors can not find what is wrong with you, they always say it's emotional. I went to the psychiatrist, who wanted me to talk about oral copulation the whole hour I was in his office. There is not really that much you can say about " giving head." The next psychiatrist fell a sleep when I was talking about the high points of my life. I was alone in San Francisco, and it was very tough. I taught myself data entry and when health problems reared it's ugly head again, I moved to Las Vegas to be a taxicab driver.

MY SPELLING

Rafael posted this in April

SO YOU MAY READ CORRECTLY.

This Patty's editor is going to love her. To have to do all the work for her spelling and syntax will require major rewrite. You all keep posting as we need a laugh. Are you are the same people?

Patty: He is referring to my pen name of Gretchen Steadfast.

I wrote back on www.vegascabbie.com: Fuck You.

Bacon Bacon post this message in April.

I was responding to Rafael and then I saw this post by Patty Noland. I thought it summed up my feelings very, very well. Is he the,"know it all, opinionated cabbie that many of my passengers are always complaining about?" Hey, Rafael, you have spoiled this "truly great website" for me. I am tired of you busting bubbles. You could not brainstorm your way out of a paper sack. You have made a peaceful person like me resorts to negativity. Have you always been a "party wrecker,"or just have you always been so non-inspiring?"

Be sure to try correct my spelling. Like spelling even matters in this open public forum. You could not understand a parable if it dropped on your head.

Mr. "B" wrote this message on www.veagscabbie.con

By the way Mr. Rafael:

If Gretchen is going to write a book, why should it bother you? Why try to rain on her parade? If you knew anything about book editing, you would realize that an editor's job is to take a "diamond in the rough" and polish up the hidden brilliance.

Patty: I like the last part about me being a diamond. Dear readers: do you see what good guys the taxicab drivers can be?

Bacon Bacon; Of course, this concept is something you could not understand. Your job is to instigate people into getting pissed off. That's what you do. Right Bud? That's what turns you on. I might say you are very good at what you do. It is too bad you couldn't set a higher goal for yourself .

Patty: A few months later, Rafael sent me an e-mail and he told me that he was sorry if her hurt my feelings and,he hoped that book was a success. One morning, I was at Bellagio's and I met Rafael, and he is really nice guy. He told me that he reads www.vegascabbie.com, but he is no longer was writing to VC. Rafael saw how many of the cab driver's were getting into trouble with the taxicab owners. I told Rafael that he was a rose petal waiting to be plucked.

I received this e-mail from Duke who worked tor for the The Las Vegas Tribune, I had spelled Los Angeles as Las Angleles

Thanks for the up date Gretch; I hope you have a good got a good spell checker....keep me posted. I wrote back to Duke,"Einstein could not spell."

Duke "Einstein did not have a computer equipped with a spell check either, but never the less, I am really excited for you and I not wait to see a copy of the manuscript.

CHAPTER SIXTEEN
TAXI LAND

Old time driver's play cards in the pit. Some of the cabbies sleep in their cabs, and how they sleep is beyond me.

At work, we have an Ethiopian supervisor cab driver. Shawn is the hippest person at the cab company. He understands American lingo, and he can swear in English. Since, I am always raising hell around Frias, broken down cabs and such, I wanted to go to talk to Charlie Frias, Shawn saved me one day because he knew I would just get fired.

Since, Mr. Frias was taking four dollars and fifty cents a day for the up keep of our cabs, I would like to talk to Charlie, because the mechanic's are taking Mr. Frias to the cleaners.

Shawn works from three am to seven am as a supervisor and then he goes to work as a taxicab driver until four pm.

We have my favorite car 1810, it breaks down every time I take it out. The mechanic at Frias told me not to pay attention to the car until smoke is coming out the of engine

I saw Hound Dawg at work and he told me that he needed an operation for arthritics in his knees. He is putting off the operation, hoping that there is some miracle cure. I told him to throw away the brace, stop mixing the yeast with water, and sticking it up ass, and have the operation.

I am a terrible taxicab. One day, I left my taxi permit at home. This is the picture we have in our car to identify us. My work number is 1892, so I drove the cab 1892 home. (It sounds reasonable) I had the wrong cab, to appreciate this mistake; I was now driving a stolen cab. When I returned to work, my supervisor, Steve was beside himself.

Susie Q. does not know Las Vegas. If someone gets in her car, and they give her an address and they do not know where they are going too, she tells her customer, "if you don't know where you are going, and I do not know where I am going, "you had better take another cab."

Susie Q. once dropped customers off at a strip club. She usually drops off , but she does not pick up. Two guys jumped into her cab, one of the customer's had his hair dyed three different dolors, orange, blue, and red. He had all of this jewelry in his ears. He said to Susie Q, "All of the girls in Las Vegas suck." Susie Q. replied "clean yourself up, take off all the jewelry, get rid of those stupid colors in your head, and maybe you will get a girl. I mean, look at yourself."

Once, at the MGM, Susie and I were talking and John had to blow his whistle twice. I told John not to ever bother us when we are talking.

In the last two weeks, my car has broken down four times. I hope that I am not repeating myself, but we do not get paid for down time. I was at the MGM, and my car wouldn't start. The MGM has a divider between the drivers and driveway, so the hotel cabs can stage there. Two drivers had to push my car so that I would not be in their way.

I went into work at 5:30 in the morning and my steering wheel would not turn over. The taxicab driver who had driven the car the night before, could have come in an hour or so earlier, and had his cab fixed, but he was with his love of his life, making money. I took another run down cab, and it was getting hot in Las Vegas.

When I came back to the yard, a taxicab driver was learning how to be a supervisor, (he will be fired shortly) he asked me how the air-conditioning was working? I replied to him, " it was not that bad, if you leave the doors and the windows opened." He told me, "go to the mechanic's and have the car fixed."

Most of the other taxicab drivers will not make it easy for you, if you try to get in front of them in a line at a stand, they will kill you. The first day, I started to work, I went up to the Rio Hotel, and I drove right up to the door, a taxicab driver started yelling at me. I told him that it was my first day, and he gave me the high sign. It would seem to me that the taxicab companies should add a day to your driving and tell you the do's and dont's of the cab business in Las Vegas. The T.A. Should make sure you can drive. (Well, there goes me driving a cab.)

Susie Q works from four in the morning until two thirty in the afternoon. She told me that she hates the sun. I asked her, "why did you come to Las Vegas?" She told me that, " she was going through a mid-life crisis."

One morning at the MGM, a cab driver had already made forty dollars. The rest of us wanted to know how he had managed to do this with only two rides. He said when a "customer has only a one hundred dollar bill to pay his fare, he tells his client, he does not have change, and he asks his customer, " how much money do you want back?"

For example, if the fare is only six dollars and the customer wants ninety-two dollars, the bad taxi driver tells him to go into the airport and get the money. He has to leave his luggage in the car, and the meter keeps running. If the customer tells the cabbie that, " he wants eighty dollars back, you make the change for him.

I don't know, it seems to be pretty shady to me.

There is a new regulation in the strip clubs. You cannot touch the dancers, put money down their G-strings, nor have any dancer that has fallen in love with you do any more then lap dancing. When a strip club dancer sits in your lap, and does her thing, a dancer can make a hundred dollar an hour,

The new rule is the dancers can take men into a private room. The strippers have to make sure the room is visible to the vice cops. Dear Readers, can't you just see it now? One cops says to his partner "John, I think that gentleman put his hands on Helen's breast. Should we let them finish or arrest him now?"

Patty: There isn't any way that this bill is going to pass.

After September 11th the mayor of Las Vegas said that he wants more men to "go to the strip clubs and partake in lap dancing." Mayor Goodman also said, "I have never had a lap dance."

THE SNITCH

Taximan 696 posted this message in August on www.vegascabbie. com

"I was on the nut at the Rio Hotel, and four guys came up to me to go to the Palms Hotel. The valet right in front of me started acting as a doorman, he sold them four passes to "Rain" for forty dollars.

After I delivered my passengers to the Palms, I went directly to the manager at the Rio, and told him of this incident. The manager along with the security guard, went straight to the "valet/doorman and confronted him, he is no longer is working at the Rio.

In appreciation of my assistance, I received a stack of VIP line passes with free admission to the club Rio. "Guys, if you bitch to the right people, you do get results."

Patty: What a prick this guy is! He could have said something to the doorman, but to get this guy fired is malicious to me. You have heard all through my book about taxicab drivers being taken advantage of by doorman and customers.

Why should you feel sorry for drivers when they pull something like this on a doorman.

Mushier posted this message in August

So, let me get the straight. You got a doorman fired for not doing exactly what you wanted to do? Somebody beats you to the punch and loses his job? You are out of your mind. I really hope he doesn't have kids to feed.

Patty: Right now is a bad time to be out of work. If all of these doormen treated cabbies the same way, turning in every violation they see, most of the cab drivers' would be losing their jobs on a weekly basis. It kills me that the cab drivers live in their world that says only taxicab driver can make forty dollars at one shot

I have made some mistakes in my life. I should have never married my first husband. I should have never had the affair with the guy in construction, never run off with the crook, I should have passed on the fireman, passed on the hippy, and the guy that owned the fish company. However, with Jack owning the fish company, at least, I received all of my fish free. I

The biggest mistake that I have made was leaving Yellow Cab, at least there is stability and continuity at Yellow Cab, We had to wait eighteen months for health benefits, but who cared? I would just sit there at Union Cab swearing at myself, "Why did I leave."

I quit Yellow Cab due to an argument over a fare. The story goes like this. a customer wanted to go to Henderson, and the trip is a good fare, and it costs twenty-six dollars . When we arrived in Henderson, she told me to wait for her which meant, I left the meter running. She said that she had to go to a meeting, and it was very important for her to be on time. When my customer came out of the bank, the cab would not start. It took thirty thirty minutes to get another cab. I called my supervisor, and told him that I was not going to charge my customer the extra fifteen dollars. She was depending on me to get her to her next destination. He told me that " she would pay, or I would pay.

I decided to quit. I went into the office, and I told Dave that I was quitting. Dave said to me, "No you are not." He signed off the extra fifteen for me.

The truth of the matter, is that I was in a lot of pain driving cars with three hundred thousand miles. What I should have done was go talk to Bill about my situation and have Bill put me in a van. At the time, I did not realize that being in a van would make all of the difference in the world. They treated me like the "Queen of the Hop," at YCS. So, if anyone comes to Las Vegas, and wants to go to work as a taxicab driver, just mention my name to Bill at Yellow Cab, he will put you to work immediately.

I, also missed Bob.

Once, some people from Yugoslavia wrote a letter, telling me I was the best cab driver in Las Vegas. I had given a copy too Bill and he told me that he would put in it my file.

After I quit, I asked Nichols about my letter. She told me, "the letter was not there in my file."

When Nichols husband, who also worked at YCS, received a complimentary letter, it was put all over the place.

HELEN IS STILL TELLING ME WHAT TO DO

When I was working at Union Cab, Helen was a supervisor at Yellow Cab. One day, I was in the tunnel at Bellagio's Hotel, and I could not get my car into parking gear.

This cab was older then fire. I rolled back and almost hit another car. Helen told me that a driver, who was behind me had come up and told her about my driving. Get this; the driver was not even a Yellow Cab driver. I guess the taxicab driver was so concerned about me that he felt he had to go to Helen.

I went to the Aladdin Hotel and I was trying to back up. What a laugh? Helen was behind me, and she gave me the word, "you should not try to back up anymore." (Isn't that a brilliant observation.)

I was up at the Paris Hotel, and I was coming up a line that drivers do not normally use. I do not remember the exact reason I was in this line, I thought it was because Scott or Charles, the door men told me to "move up." Helen was right next to me and she made a point telling me, "you are not suppose to be in the lane."

On one occasion, my cab had smoke coming out of it. I was in such a rage, that I went back to the yard. I was yelling that I wanted to speak to the boss, Charlie Frias. I over heard a new supervisor, who had been in the cab business for three and half months, (like Sarah Palin) speaking to one of the immigrants cab drivers, as if he had all of power over them. I think his words were something like this, "Do you want to go home?"

I must have said something to him, because he was sarcastic to me. I told him,

"Don't talk to me like you do to the immigrants. You had better be respectful to me, or I will have my union representative down here in five minutes." (Since I was not in the union, it was rather outrageous for me to call on the union.) "I do not ever want to hear you talking that way to immigrants, or for that matter, to anybody. They have enough problems without some seven dollars and fifty cents an hour, flunky supervisor, giving them a bad time. Next time, I hear you speaking this way, I will have your job.

This supervisor said something to me which was so stupid, that I could not believe my ears.

Dummy: It is the drivers' fault when a car breaks down.

Patty: It has nothing to do with the facts that the owners do not take care of the car, and hire anyone that is a good mechanic. I was talking to my brother-in-law, Joe, Joe, the Greek, who works for Lucky Cab Company (the best cab company to work for) He said to me, "Don't the mechanics have to be certified?"

Patty: We are lucky if the foreigners have a green card.

My friend, Jan told me that this gentleman in her car, was jacking off. When he came, he tried to squirt the "come" on her, so, that it would ruin her dress. (Nice, huh)

A taxicab driver tried to "long Haul" Jan's mother. He picked up Mom at the Fiesta Casino and drove her on the freeway, and God knows where else. When he arrived at Jan's house, the bill was for thirty-four dollars. When Jan came out, and she heard how much the cab bill was, she laughed and told the driver it was a ten-dollar ride, and that was all she was not going to pay him. This extra twenty-four dollar fare, the driver was going to have to pay to the cab company at the end of the day. The driver had given Jan's mother his card. When

Mom wanted to go to Fiesta Casino, Jan called the taxicab driver and asked the driver if he would come back to pick up her mother, he refused. (After all, taxicab drivers have some pride when they get caught stealing.)

Another driver picked up a girl that was getting married. She and all of her friends were going to a Latte party at the Chippendale's. About ten good looking guys were doing their thing. Apparently, the bride had gotten loaded because she was giving, "head," to one of the dancers in the show. All of her friends were taking pictures to give to her grand children, or so the story goes.

I was at the Crazy Horse, there was an argument out side of the Horse and the policeman told me to take the stripper home. Her husband, the pimp was being taken to jail. She started crying telling me that her marriage was over. She decided to go back to the Crazy Horse and jumped out of my cab.

A taxicab driver brought in his cab two hours early because the car was sick. He had the mechanic put a work order in the car because the brakes needed to be fixed. When the night driver came in, he threw the work order out of the car, because, he did not want to lose any time driving. Jack sent this guy home for a few days when he found out about this breach of good faith.

I had a male friend who was a taxicab driver, and he was tired of the whole thing, plus he was quiting, or getting fired from every taxi cab company in Las Vegas. I asked him, "Why don't you just go down to the local strip clubs for men, and just take off your clothes.

Pancho told me, "I will take this job offer under advisement."

I was at the Venation Hotel and I was trying to turn off in a lane that we are only suppose to go through when there is not cabs staging. I pulled up in front of a car that was already in the lane. (In another wards, I was jumping the line.) She practically came unglued. She started screaming at me. She told, "me that she had seen me around, and I knew the rules.

Damn, the long dresses. She ran up in front of me, and told the taxicab driver, and he agreed with her. (She was a very pretty girl.) She wanted me to do three days in the electric chair.

Pablo Cruz is the Dear Abby of Las Vegas. All problems with immigrants, driving a cab, your love life, gambling, call Paul, during his working hours at Bellagio's, when he is loading five drunken gamblers who have won money.

Right in front of the taxicab company sits a gentlemen in his Cadillac loaning money to the taxicab drivers. He calls his company the, "Loan Doctor." It must be worth his while because he is there everyday.

I had two gentlemen in my car that told me that they were from Florida that said to me, " we have just gotten married." They kept asking me about the gay bars in Las Vegas. I was not even going to even get involved in this number.

People often tell their problems to bartenders, hair dresses, and taxicab drivers. I was giving a gay gentleman a ride in my car and he told me how difficult it was when he was growing up. He had a partner and they had to rent a two bedroom house so that his family or bosses would never realize that he was gay. If a piece of paper means so much to Gays, let them get married.

Dan E-mailed me on something personal that I had said about myself.

I always have worked days, because I am terrified to be late. I would have to go to bed every night by 7:30 pm to make it to my four o'clock in the morning shift. I have such an aversion of being late that one time, I woke up, and it was day light outside. I thought, "I am late." So, I called Bob at YCS, he told me, "it was still the same day. This happened to me twice. My Father always told me, "If you are late, it is like telling someone that your time is more important than their time.

Dan: This is the kind of stuff you should put in your book. In fact, I'm going to put in my next article. I'll send you a copy when it come out.

I picked up a crippled man at Bellagio's and he refused help getting into my car. He told me that he was a tax attorney in Washington DC. I really thought that he was amazing.

In the back seat of my car, I found a hundred dollars, being the most honest person in the world; I went into the YCS and ask the cab drivers if they had lost a hundred dollars? Do you know that at least tens drivers told me that the money was theirs. I found it hard to believe all of the cabbies, so I kept the money for myself. We more of less have a rule that if someone leaves money in your cab, and you do not remember your fare, you can keep the money for yourself. Most all of the cab drivers do not have good memories.

In the winter time, the temperature drops down to twenty eight in the night time. I told some people from Michigan about this, and they said to me, "Boo, who, poor you.

There was a man in my car from New Zealand. He left his wallet, passport, all of his money, airplane ticket, and his traveler's checks in my car, I do not pretend to be completely honest, but I had visions of him getting to the reception desk and realizing that he had lost everything. I called dispatch, and dispatch told me that he was waiting for me at the Flamingo Hotel. When I gave him his wallet, he seemed so relieved, and he gave me twenty dollars.

I picked up a couple at Bellagio's Hotel. He did not realize that I was a taxi cab driver, and he told me to get into the cab. She looked to me like she was a "lady of the night." She did not say a word to me. When we arrived at the Executive Airport, my savior, came around the taxi to me and told me that "I had taken good care of him and tipped me twenty dollars. I almost said to him,"When you come back, I will be waiting here for you."

One morning at Bellagio's, a gentleman was trying to rent a limo, you can not use a Bellagio's limousine unless you are staying there at the hotel. He was passing out twenties, "Nick the Greek told me that he worked at the Club Paradise.

I went to the Paradise every day for a week, looking for Santa Claus. All I could find there was a reindeer.

I picked up a girl one morning, who was going to Australia, she told me that she had been married the night before.

Patty: Where is your husband?

Carolyn: My husband left me with in a few hours.

Patty: What did he say?

Carolyn: He can not handle marriage.

Patty: How long have you known this guy?

Carolyn: About three years.

Patty: The worse scenario is that she gave up her apartment in San Francisco. She had a low rent contract. (Me, always thinking about money.) Can you get your apartment back?

Carolyn: No.

Patty: The potential husband naturally knew about the apartment. He is a bastard.

What goes around, comes around. I do not pretend to be the most honest taxicab driver, but I picked up two girls from the airport going to the Venetian, I had a fifty dollar bill. When we arrived, she gave me a hundred dollar bill. I gave her the change thinking that the fifty dollar bill was a twenty dollar bill. And off she went.

CHAPTER SEVENTEEN
HOW I MAKE MONEY NUMBER TWO

If my customer's are from Germany, I always tell Boris that I was in Germany when the Berlin Wall came down. Germany is so clean compared to Russia, I always feel like telling the Germans that they won the war.

If I have customers who are from Omaha, Nebraska, I say that Johnny Carson Henry Fonda and Malcom X. are from Nebraska. Marlon Brando also studied acting in Omaha.

If you are from Connecticut, Phil Donahue and his wife live there, also David Letterman.

When my customers are from Sacramento, California, I tell them that I have lived there. (My God, is there a place where I haven't lived?) I understand that many people who work in San Francisco, are commuting from Sacrament to San Francisco. These drivers are on the road four hours a day.

Seattle, Washington. I tell my lovely customers that Seattle is the most beautiful place in the United States. When I was up in Seattle, you could go down to Pikes market, and park all day for one dollar and fifty cents.

If you are from Boston, I always ask my customers about the, "Big Dig?" This is the construction going on in Boston to bring public transportation system to the natives. The builders were so corrupt that they stole everything they could get their hands on. One truck driver came into the site everyday and filed up his truck with steel. Everyone was fired. I usually say to my Boston riders, "I hope the previous manager who is now living in the Bahamas is having a wonderful time.

Bermuda: Tell me about off shore banking?"

England: When the American soldiers were in London, during World War Two, this is their quote: They are over paid, overfed, oversexed and over here."

Patty: Some how this quote makes me uneasy, and makes me angry.

Once, I had a London cabbie in my car. He told me that most drivers in England own their own cars. John has to pay two thousand pounds a year for his insurance. He would like to come to Las Vegas and work, so he wouldn't have this responsibility. I told John, "we would love to have you." He replied, "but I am English." I told him, "he could marry me, get his citizenship papers and then divorce me and bring his wife over to the United States." He also told me, "Americans, and prostitutes are the best tippers in the world."

CHAPTER EIGHTEEN
MURDER AT THE CRAZY HORSE TOO, AND BUFFALO JIM

In April of 2008, Buffalo Jim died, either by murder or by natural causes. I have a hole in heart .

1. Jim went to a motel by himself, which obliviously means he was meeting someone.
2. He was set up. The hooker said that he was having a heart attack. If she was trying to protect herself, why didn't she just call the medics from the lobby or right outside of the motel? Jim was well aware of some of his enemies trying to catch him with a girl. Jim was married up until a few years ago, and Jim took care of all of his children, had breakfast with the kids every day, and then after a hard day's of work, he would come home to his children. When my first book came out, Jim had me personally sign a copy for his youngest daughter.

I knew that Jim had been receiving death threats. I had talked to Jim a few months before he died, and he did not sound good, and I thought maybe he had been working too hard.

All Jim had in his pocket was one dollar. This is a old Mafia trick, apparently, a lot of people feel that Jim was murdered. I E-mailed Steve on December 23, 2008.

Dear Steve; I was told that Jim was driving someone else's car, and he wasn't suppose to being to this according to Law Number One, of criminal life in the big city. I do not understand the car part, and maybe you can explain this to me.

Steve: Buffalo had repossessed Bob Stupak's 1974 Rolls for non-payment of a twenty thousand dollar repaid bill. On the night of Buffalo's death, he was driving that car. Buffalo also had a 1974 Rolls, same color, that at first was thought to be the car he was driving on April 5.

There were five hundred people at his farewell, and the funeral ran the gambit of society.

This next article is the true story about a good guy, Buffalo Jim, who is Elvis Presley, tap dancer, Liberace, Good Samaritan, stand up guy, and public servant. Quote: Every man has to test himself, and if he was courageous, and lucky, he found maturity. This was all the reward you could ask for, or were entitled to; growing up. By Work Just, The translator (1991).

CAST OF CHARACTERS:

Steve Miller:	Investigating reporter for Las Vegas Tribune.
Rick Rizzolo:	Owner of Crazy Horse Too.
Rick Rizzolo Attorney:	Dean R. Patty,
Bart Rizzolo:	Father of Rick Rizzalo.

Patty: This one you will love; Reverend Dr. Annette Marie Patterson Rizzolo: Minister of Universal Church for Life Enhancement, sister of Rick Rizzalo.

Crazy Horse Strip Club:	Strip club where beatings and murders supposedly went on.
Mr Scott Fau:	Victim
WHTNESSES	FRIENDS AND FOES.
Vinny:	Manager of Crazy Horse Too Strip club.
Christ Johnson:	Victim
Maurice, "Mo," Mckenna:	Bouncer at Crazy Horse.
Attorney: Michael Silverman:	who does not want to be identified.

Witnesses for Buffalo:

David Beamis

Robert L. Wesphall

Michael Paraaquests

Mayor Goodman, ex mayor of Las Vegas. (I liked him.)

Kirk Henry:	Victim, now a quadriplegic
Renatta Schiff:	Owns property on Industrial Blvd, where Crazy Horse Too Strip Club lives. Also has a restaurant in Green Valley.
Don Sottles:	Boyfriend of Renata Schiff

At the Crazy Horse Too, a customer was kicked out of the club. The bouncers took him out into the parking lot and in front of a large crowd, beat him close to death. He manged to walk to the railroad tracks, not far from the Horse, and died.

It was four in the morning, when Mr. Fau got into a beef. He had probably been gambling and he was drunk when he arrived at the Horse.

You would think that all strip clubs would have some sort of policy towards drunks, like hanging them or strangling them to death. A witness to all of the beatings at the Horse, was Mr. Kennedy, who had a business next door. He complained about all of the sex that was going on in the parking lot, plus the drugs.

Patty: I don't mind the sex or drugs, it is the kicking someone to death that catches my attention.

This is an article that Steve Miller wrote for the Las Vegas Tribune.

I am sorry that I do not have the date.

RIZZOLO EXPLAINS WHAT HAPPENED.

Regarding Kirk Henry's broken neck, Mr. Rizzolo wrote, "Mr. (Steve) Miller also refers to another alleged beating that occurred at my club on September 20,2002. No "beating occurred at my club on that day."

Patty: On that day? How many beating have taken place at the Crazy Horse? It sounds like there has been more then one beating.

Rick: A customer leaving the club drunk did trip, but in no way was he beaten. About the only accurate fact reported by Mr. Miller was the club personnel were standing over the injured man. Of course, Mr. Miller does not mention that my employees were assisting the injured man, as that would ruin his insinuation that my employees had beat this man. Regarding, Scoot Fau's death, Mr. Fau was not even dead when he was found.

Contrary to what Mr. Steve Miller chooses to report, the coroner, who examined Mr. Fau's body could not determine the cause of death but completely ruled out that Mr. Fau was beaten to death or that his death was cause by an altercations, Mr. Fau, with his friend had come into the Crazy Horse Too in an inebriated state, threatened and harassed my bartender. When my employees were attempting to eject Mr. Fau, who was at least six feet tall and weighed three hundred pounds from the club, Mr. Fau took off his belt, wrapped around his hand, and struck one or more of my employees who eventuality had to go to the hospital for these injuries.

The police had to be called in and it was the police who ejected Mr. Fau from the premises and saw these two people walked southwards away from the club. At least three hours had elapsed before, Mr. Faus' body was found on the train tracks from the Crazy Horse.

Steve Miller says that, "It will be up to the truer of fact in both cases to determine the validity of Mr. Rizzolo explanation.

300 HUNDRED BOUNCER TO BE TRIED FOR BATTERY.

Nine Beatings Reported – Pattern of Violence continues.

Steve Miller wrote this article for the Las Vegas Tribune

A 300-pound, 6'1" man employed as a bouncer at the Crazy Horse Too Topless Bar, at 2476 Industrial Road in Las Vegas is scheduled to be tried January 29 in Municipal Court on two assault and battery charges.

Maurice "Mo"McKenna, 41, was citied but not taken in to custody in May, 2002, for the alleged beating of Scottsdale, Arizona tourist Michael Silverman. This was the second citation McKenna has recently received for allegedly beating Crazy Horse Too patrons.

Silverman's attorney told the Tribune that his client was waiting for the court results of the two battery cases before deciding whether to file a civil complaint against McKenna and his employer, Frederick Rizzoli, owner of the Crazy Horse Too.

The attorney, who wished not to be identified, said that he expects the judge to order McKenna to take impulse control counseling, but because Mo McKenna has had another similar charge a dismissal is not anticipated. The attorney said that McKenna has a history of violet behavior.

Patty: I cannot blame the attorney for not wanting to be known, anyway he is living in the Samoan Islands. I feel that Mo should forget about anger management class, because it's too late for him.

Steve: Mckenna has also been identified as the bouncer who allegedly assaulted Glendale, California tourist. Christ Johnson on Monday, October 21. Johnson in a police report stated that a Crazy Horse bouncer, Mo, pushed him into the street where he fell twisting his ankle

Johnson told the Tribune that the man who pushed him weighed over 300 pounds and matched McKenna description.

Patty: In other wards, you do not want to bring Mo home for dinner to meet the folks.

I received this e-mail from Janelle Ramos in November, who is the owner of the The Las Vegas Tribune.

Subject: Re. Murder at the Crazy Horse Too.

Dear Patty:
I have only been able to directly view parts of your manuscript. One question on these parts of your book,,you put large sections of text that are copyrighted from the Las Vegas Tribune. Did you obtain WRITTEN permission from the paper to use their articles?

Patty: I must admit that the E-mail scared me. How did Mr. Ramos see part of my manuscript? I guarded my book like it was the "crown Jewel." By the way, Dear Readers, Steve had given me permission to reprint any of his articles.

The next article is about Buffalo Jim who has been in a fight with Crazy Horse for years. I went down to meet Buffalo Jim, he is a huge man with a long beard, he used to be a pro-wrestler. His office is unbelievable, as there are papers everywhere. Jim gives his customers' the best and cheapest service possible.

I had a quote from an auto repair shop some where else in Las Vegas. The mechanic told me that it would cost thirteen hundred dollars to fix my car. Since my car was only worth about five hundred dollar, I was looking for a cheaper mechanic. Jim fixed my car for around four hundred and fifty dollars. As far as I am concerned, he is one of the most honest, sweetest gentlemen that I have ever known. He has pictures of all of the pro-fights that he has fought. He is always on the phone so you have to try to talk to him while he is fending off all of the phone calls that he receives from people. Smart people take their cars to Jim's to get their auto's fixed.

Crazy Horse Too had the audacity to move next door to Jim's shop where Buffalo Jim had been on the site for ten years. Jim put a huge buffalo in front of his shop. The buffalo drove the owners of the Crazy Horse insane as they were trying to create a facade of sophistication, believe me, this statue was not small. The Landlord, Renatta Schiff made Jim kill the buffalo.

CRAZY HORSE AND BATTLE OF LITTLE BIG HORN

Steve Miller featured this article on August 1st. 2001 for the Las Vegas Tribune.

In 1876, the battle of Little Big Horn, (Custer's Last Stand) was considered one of the biggest blunders in military history, resulting in the extermination of two hundred and sixty-six men, including Lt. Col George Armstrong Custer.

Patty: This blunder was before George Bush took us to Iraq.

Steve: In 1997, the Nevada Department of Transportation issued an environmental impact statement on the widening of Industrial Road to six lanes. The project is expected to commence at the completion of the Sahara Avenue, 1-15 over pass reconstruction that is presently underway.

The widening of the road to over one hundred feet is expected to cause major hardships for several adjacent property owners, including the taking of some driveways and entrances now fronting the roadway. One of the properties expected to be affected is a strip center owned by Renata Schiff, a successful restaurateur and proprietor of the upscale Renate's restaurant in Green Valley. Schiff's Industrial Road property is north of the Sahara over pass and includes the leaseholds of Buffalo Jim Barriers and Frederick and Frederick Rizzoli.

Patty: The strip clubs are not allowed to be one thousand feet from each other, but if they measure by Alaska's standards, the clubs have an extra two thousand feet left over.

Steve: The strip clubs affected by the Clark County Ordinance; Can Can Room, Club Paradise, Club Platinum, Baby Dolls, Deja Vu, Showgirls, Diamond Cabaret, Divas Las Vegas, Foxy Girls, Kitten Lips, Lennon's Library, Leopard Lounge, Play It Again, Sam, Pussy Cats, Sapphire, Silhouettes, Spearmint Rhino, Striptease, Wild J's Book & Video, and Crazy Horse Too.

Buffalo Jim, a Native American, has happily conducted business in his thirteen thousand feet of leased space for the past twenty-two years and has eight years remaining on his lease. He pays only forty three cents per square, a true bargain in this day and age.

Located between Barrier's Auto repair shop and his wrestling school is Rizzolo's Crazy Horse Too topless joint. Rizzolo is reported to pay Schiff much more in rent per foot than Barrier for twenty-six thousand feet of converted warehouse space and store fronts.

Rizzolo said he once offered Barrier one hundred thousand dollars to move out Barrier denies ever receiving any offers. Since the supposed offer, the hard feelings between Barrier, and the topless club owners intensified with no peace pipe in sight. Both men filed lawsuits against one another after Renata Schiff tried to evict Barrier's business. She later dismissed her action when Barrier included her in an ICON lawsuit.

Patty: I have a feeling that Rick Rizzolo, and Ms. Schiff see Buffalo Jim like a trick from the reservation.

As the lawyers continue to pour gasoline on this fiery feud, one obvious questions keeps surfacing. "Why hasn't Rizzolo, or Schiff offered to buy out the remaining years of Barrier's lease? Barrier reports that he has always been open to a fair offer. Simple mathematics may answer that question.

Barrier pays only forty-three cents per foot for space that is renting elsewhere for at least one dollar, and twenty-five cents. He also has two well-established businesses at that location. If Rizzolo, and Barrier wanted to accommodate each other's needs as gentleman, what would the fair market value to pay Barrier to move on?

Based on a comparable net for nearby commercial space, the difference between what Barrier is not paying, and what he would be paying elsewhere with a new lease is at least eight-two cents more per foot. Translated into monthly rent, it would take at least ten thousand seven hundred dollars per month in additional rent for Barrier to reopen elsewhere.

Projected over the eight years, Barrier has left to enjoy his very low rent at his present location, the difference would amount to a total $1.23 million in rent above what he is now paying. This estimate does not include his moving expenses downtown, and the cost of advertising the move to his steady customers.

Based on Rizzolo's purported offer, Barrier is not budging, and time may be running out for the Crazy Horse. Several out-of-site gentleman's club operators are presently scouting for location in the valley while two new upscale gentleman's clubs are expected to open near the Crazy Horse within a year. and Rogich's Broad Room, and Michael Galari"s " Jaguars."

It's speculated that if the Crazy Horse is unable to purchases Barrier's lease in the very near future, the entrance to the nightclub will be forced into a alley making it noncompetitive. This may open the door for the new, upscale clubs to take over the older club's clientèle.

Buffalo Jim is setting in a cat bird seat, and he knows it! He says he has no intention of selling below market value and feels he's secure with his low rent and steady business until 2008, when his lease expires.

In the mean time as this contest of wills unfolds, you may believe that Frederick Rizzolo may end up feeling like George Custer at the Battle of Little Big Horn.

Patty: Buffalo Jim asked me what the other taxicab drivers felt about him fighting this politically connected landlord. I told him that the "taxicab drivers just wanted to make money, but how could anyone respect someone who owns a strip club? It's not like Gypsy Rose Lee dancing and Mike Todd running the show."

Patty: Buffalo Jim told me that he loaned a pink antique Cadillac with eight-eight thousand miles on the car. Kid Rock wanted to propose to Pamela Anderson. Jim relayed to Rock's manager, he was not to leave town with the car. The car had not been driven over five miles since 1985.

Therefore, naturally, Kid Rock drives the Cadillac out to the desert, and the engine blows up. Kid Rock has not paid Buffalo Jim yet. I was talking to Jim around three months later, and I asked him if Kid Rock paid him.

Jim: No, but Kid Rock was in the Crazy Horse with another stripper, and he paid her ten thousand dollars for her to spend the night with him.

Patty: Now, let's look at Kid Rock's character, he does not pay his friends, and he already cheating on Pamela. I was talking to John at the MGM Hotel and he told me "I am going to call Pamela immediately."

Las Vegas Mercury Newspaper on March 31, 2002

George Knapp wrote this article.

Perhaps you are among the many who have grown sick of reading the on going feud between auto mechanic Buffalo Jim Barrier, and his neighbor, the Crazy Horse Too Topless Bar. So many stories have been written about the rise and and fall of their assorted skirmishes that it is tempting to tune them out altogether. This would be a grave mistake.

I'm telling you, this could be a movie. Buffalo vs. Crazy Horse sort of sounds like this year's "Dance with the Wolves." I do not mean some artsy-artsy morality play, providing deep insight into the human condition. This has the potential to be a gut-busting comedy, a wacky rip-shorting force in the vein of The "Birdcage" or "Used Cars." And if we could just get the two parties interested in the Hollywood angle, maybe we could put an end to a destructive saga that has gone on too long.

Obviously, nothing abut the feud has been funny to those involved. Far from it, Buffalo Jim says he has been operating his auto repair shop on Industrial Road. long before the Crazy Horse Too existed. For those new in town, Barrier is a big hearted local character and mechanic who pals round with professional wrestlers. Jim founded his own wrestling school, produces his own wrestling shows on TV, and has been know to stage a publicity stunts of two involving a 12 foot cigarette-smoking, papier-Mach Buffalo on wheels!

On the other side of the dispute is the Crazy Horse too, long regarded as the towns premier gentleman's club. It's owner Rick Rizzolo built the place from a tiny topless joint into a palace of earthy pleasures. Along the way, Rizzolo has become an influential member of the local society, known for his friendships with politicians and his generosity to local charities. Because his business requires privileged license, the last thing he needs is avalanche of negative publicity.

The neighboring businesses have been at each other's throats since day one, but the dispute has grown very nasty in the past two years. Buffalo says Rizzalo covets his leased space, and has plotted with the property owner to have him evicted. Rizzalo says he doesn't need the space anymore because he has expanded in the other direction. (To list all the accusations that have flown back and forth would require a column much longer than this one.)

Both have accused the other of sabotage, dirty ticks and violations of health and safety standards Both have called tow trucks on the other for allegedly blocking fire access lanes. Buffalo say his neighbor installed illegal electronic surveillance measure to spy on him. Rizzolo says Barrier has been illegally dumping chemicals and solvents. Hosts of states and local inspectors have been called to the property to investigate assorted alleged skulduggery. The fight has already ended up in court a few times, and more such appearances are likely.

Just to add a touch of the surreal, Buffalo has challenged Rizzolo to a winner take all wrestling contest. Buffalo has produced witness's statements alleging acts of prostitution at the Horse and accusing Rizzolo of using strong-arm tactics to intimidate witnesses. Rizzolo has denied it, and offered to take a polygraph test. He thinks Barriers is a publicity hound that is enjoying the attention, and former city councilmen Steve Miller, who certainly has been know to enjoy stirring a pot or two, is manipulating Buffalo. Buffalo won't deny, he gets a kick out of the media attention, but adds that he is fighting for his survival.

It would never happen in real life, of course, but in my screenplay of this story, the destructive feud would continue until the two sides finally realize it is hurting them both. In the spirit of comedic compromise, the final scene would feature Buffalo's wrestlers working as a bouncer at the Horse protecting the lovely ladies from unruly customers, and they would live happily ever after. Buffalo, and Rizzolo would not exactly become friends, but would agree to mutual co-existence. It has "sequel" written all over it.

Seriously, both of these guys have done good stuff in the community, and should find away to bury the hatchet. Maybe, a joint movie venture sounds far-fetched, but even talking about such a project might lead to future conversations and the healing of a few wounds. If the movie succeeds, I purpose TV sitcom spin off, in which Knappster moves into a house with three of the Crazy Horse dances as roommates."

Patty: Isn't that a laugh, moving in with three dancers but only if Mr. Nappster can change the girls every week. Aft all, we do not want him to get bored with hassling with the "flavor of the week."

Patty: This next article just shows you how dumb some people can be. Maybe Mr. Rizzoli needs to change his publicity man.

Steve Miller wrote this next article for the la Vega Tribune on June 12, 2002

CHILDREN PICKET TOPLESS BAR.

In a letter dated May 31, attorney Dean Patti, on behalf of topless bar owner, Fredric Rizzolo referred to children, and their families as "loitering," when they attend Saturday afternoon televised wrestling matches at Buffalo Jim's professional wrestling school, at 2455 Industrial Road.

The letter addressed to James Barrier, the owner of the wrestling school states: On Saturday, March 25,2002, you held an assembly at the Buffalo Wrestling School resulting in in approximately fifty (50) spectators loitering on the premises. As you may be aware, your lease dated July 29,1968, limits personal who can occupy the building at any give time, and restricts the number of hours you can operate on any given time.

The letter then threats, "This recent activity, among others, violates your lease, and constitutes ground for eviction. Should you repeat this activity without prior landlord approval, riciz,LLO, will be complied to terminate you lease.

Rizzolo on May 1 purchased the shopping center that houses the wrestling school center, both with long-term lease.

On the day in question, May 25,2002, the person accused of loitering" consisted of several dozen preteen children, and their parents who regularly attend the TV matches to cheer for their children. The TV program is aired the following Friday night at eleven PM on cable, channel 48 in Las Vegas and in several other cities.

Parents of children who attend the weekly matches claim that their kids are being discriminated against and that their attendance does not constitute "loitering." Several parents have pledged that if their families are prohibited from entering the building this Saturday, they and their children will continue to picket Rizzolo's topless bar.

"Get an insurance policy, and get a fire permit, and get a permit to-do that and, I'll let Jim do anything he wants," Rizzolo stated after several dozen children picketed his bar on June 8, and again on June 12, after being told they were "loitering" when they attend Saturday's afternoon televised wrestling matches at the BWF professional Wrestling school. Rizzolo's statement about permits, however, however, flies in the face of his own previous action.

Patty: In February, the roof finally falls on Mr. Rizzolo head. Eighty agents from the DEA, FBI, and the IRS finally have come calling. They removed computers, cash registers, files video surveillance equipment.

Now is the time for all good women to come to the aid of married men who have been caught on video tape doing what ever at the Crazy Horse.

The sister of Rizzolo, Reverend Dr. Annette Marie Patterson, (you have to be kidding.) managed to get in touch with Mr. Rizzolo who was next door in California, Rick ordered her to help prepare for the re-opening of Crazy Horse that night.

SOMETIME TIMES THE GOOD GUYS WIN.

Buffalo Jim says that he is going to take the horse and put it in a glue factory, and the buffalo's will keep on roaming.

Steve Miller wrote this next article on American Mafia on February 23, 2004.

VODOO SHIRINE, "HE"LL BE DEAD IN SEVEN DAYS."

Las Vegas – At first it was considered a joke. Then on Friday, in February, a Polaroid photo was hand delivered along with the message, "he'll be dead in seven days." The recipient was Vegas garage owner Buffalo Jim Barrier.

Wild spread rumors were that Crazy Horse Too topless owners Rick, and Bart Rizzolo had hired a Caribbean woman described as a "Voodoo person," to allegedly cast evil spells on Barrier. A witness described what he said were bizarre ceremonies attended by the Rizzolo's where the woman, while chanting would place pins in various parts of an action doll figure, Barrier gives away of wrestling matches.

Patty: The pins that the Voodoo person has been putting in Buffalo Jim's body have acted as a therapeutic prize to Buffalo Jim. He is out tap dancing, doing ballet, toe dancing and his wife is walking around with a smile on her face.

Steve: No one took the rumors seriously - until now. Barrier, a former pro-wrestler, and current sporting event promoter, has single handily stood up to Rizzolo, who has amassed a long record of alleged beatings, and the possible murder of a topless bar patron, and some who allegedly refuse to sign fraudulent credit card slips. It was Barrier that on September 20, 2001, who photographed Kurt Haney lying paralyzed in front of the bar.

An employee who attacked him just outside the front doors breaking his neck , injured Henry after a dispute over an eight-dollar tab. Barrier called 911 and proceeded to take photos. The next day, his photo appeared on the front page of a local newspaper and later on nation TV.

Because of Barrier's photos, the time and place of Henry's beating was highly publicized here by delimiting the possibility of claiming Henry arrived at the Crazy Horse with prior injuries. Barrier's eyewitness statements and photos are also instrumental in an on going attempted murder lawsuit against Rick Rizzalo, and an organized crime investigation of his business by FBI. Hence, the obvious burgeoning animosity toward Barrier.

After failing to stop the auto mechanic's criticism of his business practices, Rick Rizzalo sued Barrier for defamation of character. However, discovery in the case has been started pending results of the federal investigation.

To the obvious dismay of the Rizzolo's and their attorney, Barrier continues to photograph documents of beating at his neighbor's place of business.

According to Barrier the messenger said, "Bart wants me to give this to you. He said "you have seven days." The FBI is talking about the Chinese mob and they have a Chinese hit man coming to take you out. It is very eerie to go in there. The chanting of them sticking pins in your feet, It is getting weirder, and weirder. Bart has this giant guy with him and asked me to feel his muscles. He said he was "sending this six foot eight, three hundred and fifty pound bouncer to get you" stated the massager upon presenting the photo."

The messenger requested his name be with held for safety reasons. The blurred Polaroid lends credit to rumors that someone enacted a Voodoo type shrine in the Crazy Horse office where the doll figure of their next-door mantel reportedly stands beneath an oriental calendar supposedly used to count the days remaining in there for life.

The day following receipt of the photo, Barrier filed in part of a death threat with the FBI, who has Rizzolo's under investigation since February 20, 2003. He also filed a report with the Las Vegas Metro Police. He believes that finger prints on the photo should be of interest to enforcement officials.

Patty: Hey, Mr FBI man, how long does it take to finish an investigation?

Barrier commissioned the manufacture of hundreds of dolls in the likeness to be handed out at wrestling matches, and other special events. "How did they get matches, and other special events." "How did they get a hold of one of my dolls, he asked?" "I only give them to children and personal friends."

If the death threats are verified, this would be the second time in recent years that Bart Rizzolo allegedly threaten someone life.

The Rizzolo's are no strangers to the occult. The Reverend Dr. Annette Rizzolo Patterson is the minister of the "Universal church for Life Enhancement," and the daughter of Bart Rizzolo Patterson. In 2000, she was accused of opening the church to block insurance of a tavern license for a competitive topless club. When the ploy was revealed in the newspapers, she suddenly closed her church.

Luckily Buffalo Jim Barrier is not a superstitious man. If he were. he would have voluntarily broken his long-term lease and moved to friendlier pastures based on the animus of his neighbors, men with known ties to organized crime.

Patty: Mr. Rizzolo, nothing like advertising that you are going to kill someone. You are supposed to say, " You will go around a thousand corners and one of these days, I will be waiting for you to shoot you're fucking head off. My God, man, if you are going to be part of the mob, start acting like one.

Steve: In and effort to remove Jim to make way, for the expansion of their nightclub, the Rizzolo's purchased the shopping center to 2002, immediately issued Barrier an eviction notice. After two courts hearings, Barrier prevailed. The courts ruled he could remain in his two thousand square foot garage that he rents for forty-three cents per foot until the lease expires in 2008. Subsequently, the expansion was halted while two new much larger topless bars opened in close approximately.

Patty: I do not understand how Mr. Rizzolo could screw up so badly, particularly, when he has one of the best clubs in Las Vegas. Maybe, he felt that he can act as the Mafia did during prohibition. It seems to me that Rizzolo has some friends, and I do not mean that he operates on fear, or fear only. Why is he putting himself in to jail?

Maybe Jim is driving Mr. Rizzolo insane because a owner of an electrical shop can can bring him down. I am sure Mr. Rizzolo feels that Buffalo Jim is a non-person

Rick Rizzolo went to court for his criminal trial and was found innocent.

Well, the melody changes but the beat goes on..

CHAPTER NINETEEN
CONVENTIONS

Patty: I picked up this woman who had been putting on shows for the conventions, She told me, "How cheap unions are in Las Vegas." When she got out of the cab, her bill was six dollars and ninety cents, she gave me seven dollars. I did not say a word, because I felt that it must have been a mistake on her part. If she is reading this book, I would appreciate it if she would send me a dollar through my publisher.

I was at the convention center. A cab emptied in front of me, so I thought it was OK for me to follow him. A convention guard came running up and told me that I could not park in the other lane. Once you drop off, you always hope that you can pick up a ride at the same place, but this guard was making me leave the convention center without a fare. I told him that I wanted to go up the line to pick up; the guard was letting some other cabs pick up if the taxicab drivers were in the right lane.

Convention Guard: We must keep order.

The Magic convention is coming to town and about seventy thousand people will be here. When I first heard the name,"magic," I thought the conventioneers were Magicians. It turned out that the name stands for "Men's Apparel Guild in California. I was so disappointed. I thought I would have magicians teaching me tricks. (real tricks.)

One girl really made me angry. She was from North Carolina, and it was her first time in Las Vegas. I picked her up at Bellagio's Hotel, which means that she was suppose to have some money. She stiffed the doorman, and when I arrived at the Flamingo Hotel, her bill was five dollars and ten cents. She gave me, "even money," No tip. Where do these people come from? I told her that Las Vegas is a big tipping town and that she should tip the doormen. And of course, me.

CHAPTER TWENTY
TRAVELS AROUND THE WORLD AND GRETCHEN ON THE LAM

People are always asking me how I can afford such great trips all over the world. I tell my friends that I do not gamble, drink and I work all of the time. However, I must confess that I have a weakness for ice cream, so every night, I go on another diet.

On my business cards, I have put these words:

Patty Noland
Extraordinary Taxicab Driver.
World Traveler
Pro football expert.

SAN FRANCISCO

I must say something about San Francisco.

God, what fun we had in San Francisco during the 80's. I was a cocktail waitress, and I worked at a place called Roland's which was the "in spot" of the City. You could get a parking space at Fisherman's Wharf. If you went to a party, you might meet the mayor, or a hooker.

All of us would start out at Capps Corner for dinner, and then go on to Roland's for drinks where we ended up drunk. At Capps, Joe had put up all of his better customers picture up on his wall. I was naturally was up there too. A boyfriend of mine, who was jealous, told me I looked like a Mob girl friend. I wish. I was such a tramp, but a fun tramp.

I know that I could never be a crook, because I could not make all of the public phone calls. (hard of hearing.) We had a thief that was so dashing, and he had such a such a great sense of humor that every girl wanted to run a away with him. He was facing fifteen to life, and he never copped out on his partners. He was in a half-way house, and some nice bar owner put him to work as a bartender.

We had a Mexican bartender that we all loved. We use to tell Frank he should go on welfare, because he was Mexican. He agreed.

We had Joe Montana, and Steve Young. Matt Million was whispering to the New Orleans Saints about their mothers linage, and of course, the coach, Bill Walsh.

We all felt bad when Eddie De Bartelo went down, but when he copped out on Governors Edwards, saying that he did not know that Governor Edward's was bribing him, he went a little too far. What did he think the money was for "Out of commission cocktail waitresses?"

Dino Del Puente owned a bar in North Beach, and he started the first topless Club in San Francisco. Gino had a piano that would come down from the ceiling, and then go back up into the ceiling. One of his bartenders, who had to be loaded got stuck on the piano and died. (Honest to God.)

I had a great romance going on with a gentleman, who owed a fish company He was married and I could not handle the marriage parts, "laws your parents teach you, so you cannot have any fun. I feel that I had some morals in those days because if I met a man now, rich and married. I would care less.

Those were the days my friends.

RUSSSIA:When you are traveling, you have to strike when the iron is hot, I was in St. Petersburg and Moscow in 1992. In Red Square, I could not believe that a woman from San Francisco was actually walking around and viewing Lenin's body embalmed. Beautiful! At the time, the Russians loved us, but because they have not been able to convert to capitalism, we are down and out. The people feel that it is America's fault, it is nothing to do with the Mafia or corruption.

Of course, Vladimir Putin is a wonderful guy. After sitting with Bush at the Olympics, no doubt discussing their shared view of freedom in the world. Putin then knocked off Georgia.

I will never forget going to the soft drinks market. The woman in charge looked, "hard," but she was watching everyone to make sure that no one was trying to rob her. One night, at the hotel, we were all served a terrible dinner, the Russian tourist guide could not believe it when we did not eat all of our dinner. (Remember, the Germans saying that we do not eat everything on our plate)

I was on the subway trying to get directions in English to go back to the hotel, what I would do is write on a piece of paper, where I wanted to go too. I would ask a Russian and they would point me in the right direction. I would go about 20 steps and ask someone else. While I was on the subway, a Russia helped me in some way, I tried to tip him, but he would not accept any money from me.

BERLIN

In East Berlin. I used my brilliant way with the paper for help. When I reached West Berlin, there was man running after a pickpocket, who apparently had stolen his money. I do not know if the thief was ever caught. Please, all of my readers, be very careful with you currency, when you are traveling. When I was in Egypt the first time, a pickpocket robbed me of a beautiful bracelet.

EGYPT

Egypt is one of my favorite places in the world.

I went to Egypt is 1996. I mailed off for my first visa to the Jordanian Embassy in New York City. It cost me forty five dollars, plus a Fed-Ex charge. I then went to the Egyptian embassy in San Francisco where I was living. The visa cost me thirty five dollars, the Egyptian employees were so nice to me that they told me, that they "would drop the visa off at my apartment."

After four days, I called the embassy and told them that I would come by and pick up my papers. They told me that they had dropped off the necessary documents in my mailbox at my home.

My Landlady had a mailbox in her flower garden in her front yard. There was another drop in the gate that went into the trash. I went running home and I looked into the garbage and there wasn't any passport or visa. I felt like I was going to faint! I went downtown and asked my travel agent if "I really needed all of these documents?" Gloria said to me, "if you want to go on the trip you have to have your visa's and your passport.

I went backed to the passport agency, and I got another passport in twenty four hours which cost me one hundred dollars. I then sent off to the Jordanian Embassy for my second visa which cost me forty five dollars plus Fed-Ex charges because they had to "over night" it. The Egyptian Embassy did not charge me anything. I do not remember why I waited so long to get my passport and visa's, I think I had to get another passport because I had a Jewish stamp on my papers.

My trip to the Middle East was the greatest trip that I have under taken. I went to Jordan where the pink city was located. I met great people from Australia, New Zealand and South Africa.

On my plane trip back home, the tourist guide got us into Cairo at one AM. We had to catch our plane at six in the morning to go to Amsterdam which took about eight hours. My plane to New York City was seven hours late, and I had to go on to San Francisco. By then, I did not know where I was, but, every time, I go flying all over the world through time changes, I tell myself, never again. But. it is like child birth, you forget the pain, and you start planning your trip again. At, least, that is what I do.

GREECE:

In 1975, I went to Greece. All of Greece had been a delight during my first trip. I went to a Greek restaurant where no one spoke English. A Bohemian English man was working as a waiter interpreting for all of the waitresses.

There is an island called Santeria where you have to go by mule to get to the top of the island. A poor Greek man runs behind the mule to make sure that your mule does not fall off the mountain, and me too. I said to my Greek runner, "Who did you have sleep with to get this job?"

When I returned to Santeria in Greece in 1998, there was an elevator to take all of the tourists up the mountainside, I went to the same restaurant, all of the Greeks spoke English, the waitresses were really hustling. The next remark will greatly increase Greek Tourism. I was in Mykonos "haven for debauchery," and everyday there were ten ships trying to dock in Mykonos. All of the islands were just as busy.

BULGARIA

I was in Bulgaria and there was this great looking guy wearing leather, standing by his motorcycle. I thought to myself, "just stand there, my love, some rich woman will come by and takes you away from it all. "

NEPAL
MY ARRANGED MARRIAGE.

I became friends with a Nepalese that wanted me to go to Nepal to meet his brother who wanted to marry any American so he could come to the U.S.A. What the hell, it was a trip. If you want to appreciate America, go to Nepal. I was in the air for about forty hours. I was flying Cathy Lines between Los Angeles, and in Hong Kong, the captain got sick or died of something. We had to land in in Hong Kong. I missed my plane going to Nepal, and customers service asked me if I wanted to go to Bangkok? Since I am an old hand of flights being late, I knew Cathy would have to put me up for the night. I requested Cathy to let me stay in Hong Kong at a five star hotel.

When I arrived, it was in the afternoon, I was so tired, that I asked the clerk if I could have dinner sent to me room? (Cathy airlines picks up the tab.) You are given two tickets, one for dinner and one for breakfast. I was told that I could not have dinner in my room but I could order " breakfast sent to my room the next day." I replied to him, "I can not have dinner sent to me at night time? The clerk told me, "orders are orders." "I bet George Bush could have his food sent to him twenty four hours a day. However considering how people feel about him all over the world, he should bring a taster.

I went to the buffet, the restaurant captain told me that it was tea time and I would have to wait for another fifteen minutes for dinner time. I told the captain, "I do not care if it is teatime, buffet time or dinner time. I am hungry and I want to eat." God, these people are regimented.

The next day, I went on to Nepal,I had a stopover in Bangkok' I was in transit so I had to wait for other people who were going on to other countries. There were Moslem's men and women lying on the floor fixing their tea and so on. I wanted to take some pictures, but I remembered when I was in Jordan, and I took some pictures of people making vases. The shop owner was outraged that I did not ask her permission.

My first impression of Kathmandu was the smell, because the Nepalese empty all of their garbage into their streets. The people are so poor that all of their shops are like hovels. The men wear clothes that look like they were from Wal-Mart, 1959. The smog and the traffic are terrible: everyone rides motorcycles because they cannot afford cars and I assume, gas. I thought that I was going to some exquisite place like Laguna Beach, California. Boy, was I wrong. I usually like going to third world countries because the shopping is so great, but I never even saw a nice shop.

The plumbing killed me. There was a hole in the floor of the bathroom where you are suppose to squat. I told my intended that I could not handle this hole. He told me," to use the bathroom downstairs that the family never flushed."The maids clean the toilets everyday, Nepalese do not use toilet paper.

You should always shake hands with a Nepalese with your right hand, because they use their left hand to wipe their ass. My Nepalese family used their right hand to eat.

In Nepal, I met a gentleman who could speak good English. I pounced on him and he told me that he had gone to school in the USA. He worked days as a truck driver. He also was a manager of a MacDonald's in Texas. Another time, he worked days at the Pizza place and he worked nights delivering food. He became so lonely for his family that he moved back to Katmandu's. At first, when he got home, he thought that everyone looked dirty but after time, it did not bother him.

Patty: It bothered me.

Everything was going along beautifully until my intended tried to keep my passport.

Patty: Give me my passport:

Santosh: I will keep it safe for you.

Intended wife: I would like to have my passport.

Santosh: No, I think it would be better for me to keep your passport.

Intended wife: Give me my fucking passport. We were suppose to get married but my second husband has never divorced me. I had not seen Lar for over thirty years. I had told him, you get the divorce as I am running away with the owner of the bar. To get married, I had to have my divorce papers. Even if my husband had been a rat, I thank him for not divorcing me. My darling, Santosh wanted me to marry him right then and there. He was under the impression that my government would not investigate me. I told him that I could not go through the "ring number" because it might be hard on my husband. I mean, after thirty years, he must have undying love for me. I must tell you, Dear Readers, this ended my "hotel of happiness." Thank God."

I do not feel that Sontosh appreciated my sense of humor. He told me, "that the Prince of Napel wanted to marry someone that his family did not approve of." The Prince went and got a gun and killed his parents. I told him that "it seemed right to me." From what

I understand, terrorists are trying to take over the country. If you go to live in Nepal, you do not have to pay taxes.

MAINE:

My girl friend and I were sitting the Olive garden restaurant in Augusta, Maine.

Apparently, we had both maxed out our credit cards

Sylvia: How much do you have?

Patty: about four dollars. How much do you have?

Sylvia: About two or three dollars.

Patty: Well, what the hell are they going to do to us? We will just have to wash dishes. A woman who was sitting back to back to me in the next booth, turned around and gave me fifteen dollars! The general manager, Mr. Kotsimpulos got wind of our plight, and wrote the check off.

Unbelievable!

Let's say you need a stamp, the mail man is coming! What do you do? In Maine, you wait for the mailman, you give him the money for the stamp or stamps that you want to buy and he gives you the change. No robberies of mailmen in Maine.

We are now in a grocery store in Union, Maine, the local drunk is short fifty cents for his beer. The good Samaritan gives him the half dollar.

My favorite places:

New York City	Washington DC	St. Louis, and Kansas City in Missouri
Las Vegas	San Francisco	Seattle, Washington
London	Paris	Moscow

If you really want adventure. Go to the internet to **FREELOADERS OF AMERICA .COM** and you can go anywhere in the world to a family that whats to share their house with you. All you have to do is supply your food.

CHAPTER TWENTY-ONE
SEPTEMBER 11TH AND THE AFTERMATH

In Las Vegas, September 11th was a terrible time for everyone. Like many others, I was glued to my television set. The days following September 11th, no one could get out of Las Vegas. A woman told me there were worst places to be stuck in then Bellagio's Hotel in Las Vegas. With-in-four-days, the town just died. No one was coming in to Las Vegas. You could have stayed at Bellagio's Hotel for thirty dollars a night and they would probably up-graded you to a suite

People just wanted to get out of Las Vegas and go home. There were some renovated ways that people used to go their dwelling. A customer got into my car and he told me that he had just bought four cars, and he and his friends were going to be driving home. I asked my customer, "What business are you in?" He told me, " I am in the car business. When I get home, I am going to sell all of these cars as new." Apparently, all automobile agencies can have a certain amount of miles on a car before the car becomes a used car.

I picked up a couple that wanted to go to the Grey Hound bus depot. They were taking the bus to Los Angeles, since they were coming from Bellagio's, I was sort of worried about them. I asked Carl and his wife,:"how long has it been since you have been on a bus?" Carl told me," it has been twenty five years." She told me, "it has been thirty five years." They were treating the whole Greyhound number as an adventure. The tipped me and they were on their way.

I also took a couple of guys to the mobile homes sales lot in Las Vegas. He and his friends were renting two mobile homes at two thousand dollars a pop and driving back to New York City. One of the guys said that "he hadn't seen the Grand Canyon."

Patty: Who has?

In my cab I had a Muslim man who had conveniently become an American tell me that "Muslim men are so insecure, if a wife takes off her veil, the woman would become so excited, she would ran away with another man." How about the way Muslims treat their women? I would be bare-foot going over the Khyber Pass.

I picked up two girls who were going to the airport and one of them told me that she was schedule to go to Los Angeles on September 11th on American Airline number eleven. She left two days before and she was in Los Angeles when her plane crashed.

Because, there was hardly any business, I decided to go to New York City. I went down to the World Trade Center site.(Ground Zero.) The Center was still burning, the closest I could get to the site was a block away. This was alright with me, as the WTC was burring my eyes and made me sick. Jesus, what the firefighter and the police must have been going through.

If Las Vegas cab drivers acted like New York City cab drivers, we would be fired on the spot. I came out of my hotel, "The Portland Hotel," which by the way is a great hotel on 47th street. I was trying to get a ride, The first driver in line, "asked me where I was going." I said, "Lincoln Center." He said to me, "I can only drive in New Jersey. " The next driver told me, "I do not have the gas." The third driver just said "No."

I started yelling at him, What's is your number? If you can remember the cab number, you can call the company and complain about the driver, which I would never do. The taxi driver was stupid not to pick me up, because I am the last of the,"Big Tippers." Going to Lincoln Center was not a long enough ride, next time I will tell the cab driver that I want to go down to Canal Street, but I need to stop at Lincoln Center for a minute.

I started to e-mail a gentlemen in New York City that was a driver. I asked "John about driving a cab in NYC."

Patty: Are you at the mercy of the Taxicab Authority in New York City?

John: Most drivers own or lease their own cabs, so they so nor to hassles with the owners making money, because it is up to the driver how much he wants to hustles. The only people who rip you off, is the mechanic.

CHAPTER TWENTY TWO
THE MIDDLE EAST

There was an Iranian Music Festival in Las Vegas. I had an Iranian in my cab, and he asked me if I liked Israel? I thought to myself "Iran-Moslem's, Iranians hate Israel." So, I said, "Not particularly." This guy looked at me with a long fact. I asked if he was Jewish, and he said, "Yes." I had to change my whole strategy, "Boy, you guys really made the desert bloom."

I do not feel that there will ever be peace in the Middle East. The Palestinians perpetrate their hatred from one generation to the next generation. A Palestinian from Jordan took me to go to a refugee camp, and I told Olmert, "I would be upset if I was deported from San Francisco, where I was living at the time, but I wouldn't spend the next fifty years trying to get back to the City."

Patty: I had a Jewish man in my car, and he wanted me to take him to a Kosher restaurant which pisses me off right away. You should see how some conservative Jews act if you are out on a Friday night. They throw rocks at your car."

Patty: What do you think about the Palestinians?

Moses: They are all terrorists.

Patty: Did you know that President Begin was a member of the Irgun when he blew up the Kind David Hotel in 1948?

Patty: This is when the Jewish people were trying to end the occupation of Britain. Ninety-one people were killed in the King David Hotel, they were mostly Englishmen. "One man's terrorist's is another man's freedom fighter."

I am an atheist and I do not understand all of this fighting over some sand. Too many people have been killed in the name of God. When the Jews tell me that God gave them the land. I always ask the Jew's, if they have the lease that God gave to the Israelis?

When I was living in Israel, I was working at a shipping company, the owner said to me, "the public be damned: we will do what we think is best for or country."

In San Francisco, I have some friends from Nicaragua who had lost everything during the Contra war, Jose and his family came to San Francisco. Jose was an accountant in Nicaragua, and he became a janitor in the city and did quite well for himself. We have Unions in San Francisco and Jose made more money then he did in Nicaragua.

.

Anything that you want to know about immigration, just call Paul Cruz of Lucky Cab, he will answer all of your questions.

I am now quoting from Thomas Friedman book, "From Beirut to Jerusalem."

Three years later, they leave whatever country that Americans have been too, wondering what went wrong. I saw them come and I saw them go, and a strange group of invaders they were indeed. They arrived in Beirut like innocents abroad and they left three years later like angry tourists who had been mugged, cheated, and had all of their luggage stolen with their traveler's checks."

Patty: I can forgive George Bush for anything, but not for Iraq. He lied to the American people, and we have lost over four thousand troops, plus all of the Iraqis we have killed. No, wonder in the Muslim world, they hate us. .

CHAPTER TWENTY THREE
UNIONS IN LAS VEGAS

This is why I hate the unions in Las Vegas.

My friend from Las Vegas, Jim Talley was fired from Frias. I had been worried about him, and I had E-mailed him and this is what he said to me.

I suppose I was insubordinate to the all mighty mangers and they got even with me by getting rid of me.

What happened is that they have been harassing the drivers and one thing they do is to have your trip sheet scanned at the gate when you drive in. What that means is that the drivers get cheated out of 15 minutes a day because they still have to drive the cab in and gas it up, park it and turn the money in. All of that requires at least 15 minutes a day. If you multiply 15 minutes a day by 1200 drivers then it works out to 300 man hours they are stealing from the drivers day.

One day, I had a particularly bad day and they had one of the supervisors in the money room telling each driver: "Let me see your trip sheet?" I figured since I was on my own time, and had been off of the clock for 5 minutes that I didn't have to let them see my trip sheet. I refused and was suspended for 3 days, and fired when I had a few bad days.

Patty: Frias does not have to pay for Jim's insurance any more.

I wrote a letter to the CEO of Frias and below is the letter:

To: Mark James, CEO of Frias
Review Journal letters for the Editor
Chanel 13-investigations
Taxi Cab Authority board Members and Managers.

From: James P. Talley driver with 35 years experience, recently fired from Frias.

Concerning: Taxi drive being forced to steal from customers to keep a job

The stated policy at the Frias company is a zero tolerance for long hauling (stealing) from customers, Yet, I was fired for low book after being a driver for thirty-five years. Fifteen years of which I drove for the Frias Company.

The flooding of the streets of Las Vegas with taxis and the downturn in the economy have created a situation in which it is practically impossible for the drivers to earn a living above minimum wage honestly. Also there is a way in place to add taxis when needed but none to remove medallions when the city is extremely slow for the taxi business.

I went to the union to see if they could address the situation of me being fired. I was told Frias was not rehiring anyone who is fired for low book because the company then has to compensate the driver up to minimum wage. I called the federal wage board and they told me that they could not be involved because the salary I was receiving was well above minimum wage.

With the new management at Frias harassing drivers to make more money up to and including firing them is the actual in place policy. There have been at least 53 people fired in a very sort period of time for low book. I was told that one reason for this is that supervisors gets to share a bonus at the end of the year if the income of the company is increased. Since the driver's are all lumped into an "average," this forces an honest driver who does not steal from customers to resort to long hauling to steal to maintain the average and keep a job. Therefore, I have been to Whittlesea, YCS, and Western and they will not hire me because I have to tell them why I was fired from Friars. Without a job, I am trying to find a pro bono attorney to help me with the situation of been fired

Yours truly,
James P. Talley to #16808

Patty: Jim called the union and they told him they could not help him.

Patty: Dear Jim: I am in such a rage for this happening to you You work for years, and now they come up with this bull shit. How about your so-called friends?" You did so much for everyone.

There isn't anyway that Jim can get another job in Las Vegas, because he broke the cardinal rule; he went to the newspapers telling them that cab owners are cheating, as if anyone doesn't know it already.

The Union has no power what so ever in Las Vegas. When Mr. Poelman was fired from Yellow Cab for setting up the boycott of the Rio Hotel, Mr. Poelman was the president of the Professional Drivers Association. He had the head of their union, Ruthie of the AFL-CIO and everyone else to speak for him during the interview. There wasn't any way Bill was going to bring him back to Yellow Cab. Daryl was using the airport as his office, one day he brought in eighty three dollars. That gave Yellow cab the easy way out, because they do not like trouble makers..

If you were the Taxi Cab Taxicab authority, who would you like deal with? Five thousand illiterate (mostly) screaming cab drivers, or ten millionaire owners who would be taking you to lunch at Pietro's.

In one of my glorious post to VC, I said, "Fuck the unions in Las Vegas." (obscenity has it's place) I would have a better chance playing Black Jack, then with these unions representing us. What a laugh. A cab driver wrote into www.vegascabbie.com asking about joining the union. I replied and told him, "Do what ever you want to do, but the union will not do anything for the drivers."

Mike Warzlow posted this message in October.

Mike: Patty, your post shows how little you know about unions, and what they can and can't do. The best protection a driver can have is to be a member with a union contact. Without it you re not protected Steve La Croix was in the union and had a contact at A-Cab, he might still have a job if he wanted it.

Patty: The taxicab business in Las Vegas is a rotten business run by rotten people who mostly take advantage of people who do not have the eduction to do something else. (Now do not start telling me that you can work on computers.) We all know to make any money in Las Vegas, you have to be in a tipping position. I do not care if the Steelworkers is giving me Sundays off. The Steelworker union is a bunch of thieves.

I am ready to go on strike, because I hate the taxicab business here, and I hate Frias most of all. Just shut the fuck up about unions, if you knew anything about striking, you would have done something about it a long time ago.

CHAPTER TWENTY FOUR
TROUBLE IN PARADISE

I have been accused of using too many posts but these next one's are funny, I thought my readers would enjoy them.

It's a riot out there!

Hound Dawg posted this message on June 25.

I had always suspected that the "Can Can Strip Club"was ignoring Mustang Sally's injunction. To that, I say hats off. It is good to see that pompous bitch ignored somewhere other than in her bedroom.

Patty: Mustang Sally's is one of the whorehouses in Nye County.

Hound Dawg: That's where the niceties will end. I never knew that the Can Can Strip Club did not allow cab drivers to stage for customers. Therefore, on a slow early Tuesday at about 3:30 AM, after dropping off at the Stardust Hotel, I cruised over to Industrial road, I did not see any cabs at the Can Can.

Lets us check it out. Migra fish net walks ups and says,"ten minutes."

Remaining slugs that did not realize how bad they were being ripped off by the Door. Meanwhile, a Yellow Cab pulls up behind me. Okay, misery loves company. The drivers goes inside. After another fifteen minutes Woopie Pie said to me, "I have to leave." "Why " I asked?" "The owner doesn't want cabs here." I exchange a few more words with this clown and was about to pull away I said to myself "Fuck this, I want some answers."

Therefore, I walked in. The Yellow Cab driver is still inside at the counter. I asked the girl behind the counter who was not the best-looking broad, I had ever seen inside the place, which is not saying much, " What the hell is going on?"

Migra Fish: The owner doesn't want cabs sitting here."

Hound Dawg: Why not?

Migra Fish: Because he doesn't want cabs sitting here."

Hound Dawg: The Yellow cab driver leaves with a load. O.K, now, I'm pissed. I ask the girl who has apparently suck her way up to some position of authority. "Why is it O.K, for that driver to pick up? "

Just then: a Star driver pulls in to drop.

Migra Fish: Don't believe me just ask him. Do we lets cab sit here?

Hound Dawg: At first the driver had a puzzled look on his face and then sheepishly shook his head.

Star Cab Driver. Yah, right

Hound Dawg: I wasn't going to win this argument, so I said, "Fuck it" and left.

What we have going on at the Can Can is a few drivers; a clique of cab drivers still getting tips from the owner. Loyally brings them customers. Those guys stage there. Common sense says no driver in his right mind is going to hang around too long out of fear he might get the poor slug he conned into going there in the first place.

Patty: I feel that it is beautiful that the Can Can still gives tips to its favorite drivers, as long as I ams one of the taxicab drivers.

Hound Dawg: Why don't they want cabs sitting here? Well since, I did not get an intelligent response – silly me to expect that, I am left to speculate.

Maybe they do not want to make it too easy for the poor slugs to leave. Maybe, they don't want to draw attention to themselves by having too many cabs lined up, or maybe, it a secret society of drivers who, on numerous occasions, sell their passengers down the river just to collect the bounty at the other end, and as an added reward, they get the exclusive rights to stage there.

God bless the establishment who have thumbed their noses at this injustice and has attempted to continue to help us out. They are taking a big risk and how do we reward the clubs that could not hold on? We stop promoting them altogether. We divert passengers from our former friends to whomever is still paying the bounty. The Can Can Strip club was the best-kept secret out there and a gold mine for those few drivers who knew.

Patty: Thanks to Hound Dawg, Pete and all the authorities will know about this tipping. Just because Hound Dawg is not getting any money, he has to snitch on the Can Can.

The "Rookie" posted this message in June.

We all know what the Dawg is or do we?

He is one of those Doberman s, you know the ones that turn on their own master because, there is miss breeding, their skulls slowly collapse on their brain, causing them to go insane. So, bewared of the Dawg, he will even bite the hand that feeds him and this is a BIG hand. Dawg was just pissed that the Yellow driver got the ride,and he did not, maybe the Yellow cab driver was just gaming him. Who knows and who actually cares.

Patty: The Taxicab Authority will care. Hound Dawg does not seem to realize or care that the Can Can was breaking the "no tipping" law suit."

Ray Schultz resigned from his post as a Co-host on Hound Dawg's show. Ray disagreed with the Dawg's friendship with Pete. I personally felt that Hound Dawg makes as much money from his web site and gets all of the advertisers he wants on his show. Even if it's with the devil, the name of the game is money, but Hound Dawg does not realize how many friends in the taxicab business he will be losing by taking money from Pete.

This is a reply to Hound Dawg's previous post:

Help me out, Lord, can this possibly be happening? Here I thought we were all going in the same direction at the same time,and now the Dawg's drops a bomb on us? Just when the herd's is gathered here, comes the thunderstorm. Where is this post? Buried? Am I missing something? Please, Dawg, point this out to me so I can either become involved and committed or give up on you people and your scattered, insignificant bullshit forever.

Hound Dawg was fired and gave his web sit to Yahoo. From what I understand all of his advertisers vanished on him which means, Pete from Yellow cab. Pete just byes his time, and pounces on taxicab drivers that try and talk up for the drivers.

Hound Dawg's wife is working for a Seven Eleven. Hound Dawg made a lot of enemies from some of the remarks he made toward the other drivers. John and his wife are planning on moving to Florida. As for myself, I felt that Hound Dawg had a good idea with VC, but the owners 's who are way above Dawg in business just used dawg until they could get rid of him.

George was having a beef with one of the managers at his company. And he quit. George sent me an e-mall that will crack you up.

Yesterday I went over to Nellie's cab and gave them the phony application with all my Father's information on it, and used my father's name, Francisco. They took copies of my social security card and DL and my printout. If they check it out, it's all legal except our socials are different. I hope I get hired. I had on sunglasses and it was hot out.

Patty: My health had not been good and I e-mailed George, and I said to him. "How am I going to be able to go to Iraq to straighten everything out.

George: Instead of going to Iraq, why don't you just chop off your head and send it to President Bush.

A-Cab has really been getting it from all of the taxicab drivers.

JOBS OPENING FOR THE POSITION OF A-CAB

The requirement for the position of General Manager at A-Cab Company

1. An applicant cannot have more than two months of taxi industry experience
2. An applicant must be a personal friend or a relation of the owner.
3. An applicant cannot have any people skills.
4. An applicant must have a fu$k you, take it or leave it attitude.
5. An applicant must believe that being the boss makes him the boss all the time.
6. An applicant cannot have any knowledge of any state or federal labor laws.
7. An applicant must not be able to accept help or advice from an employee who has more experience, or working knowledge of the taxi industry.

Based on the above requirements it appears that A-Cab already has the best person or the job.

Patty: If you lie, or take advantage of people in business, they will do you in eventually. I use to watch Bob at YCS, and at Union, he knew everyone's name and he was always polite.

CHAPTER TWENTY-FIVE
THE END

I knew that the Taxicab Authority was going to sink under it's own power. The TA have been disgraced, " Mr. Get Me Out of Here, the president of the agency has been accused of being the boyfriend of Eva Braun, Hitler's girl friend. Lucy Lick a Lot is Oscar Wilde.

I have been nominated to be the President of the Taxicab Authority.

The first order of business is to make all of the owners of cab companies drive a taxicab with three hundred, and fifty thousand miles on the car for a year.

I E-mailed Steve La Croix, and asked how he was doing? He replied, "I know the taxicab business in Las Vegas well enough to know when it is time to get out."

It has been rumored that I am on the "hit" list by owners of the strip clubs, the Taxicab Authority, the owners of the taxicab companies, the FBI, the drivers' and let's not forget my ex-husband.

So, I am leaving for greener pastures.

My Dear Reader's, Thank you for reading my book.

COPY RIGHTS

Tipping in Las Vegas: Las Vegas Sheet Magazine July 23,2003.

George Knapp	Taxi driver's accent becomes impenetrable. Las Vegas Mercury Newspaper, 2002.
George Knapp	Buffalo Jim, March 31, 2002, Las Vegas Mercury Newspaper.
Jeff German	Taxicab Authority Chief Has His Hands Full. April 5, 2002 for the Las Vegas Journal Newspaper.
Jeff German:	Eliades Begins Fights To cabbies. April 12, 2002, Las Vegas Sun Newspaper.
Jeff German:	Olympic garden Accuses Palomino of Luring customers.
Steve Miller:	Rizzolo explains what happens. October 30, 2002 Las Vegas Tribune
Steve Miller:	300 Pound bouncer to be tried for battery. November 13, 2002, Las Vegas Tribune.
Steve Miller:	Crazy Horse and the Battle of Big Horn. April 2, 2002 with the Las Vegas Tribune.
Steve Miller:	Children Picket Topless bar, written in June 12, 2002 for the Las Vegas Tribune.
Steve Miller:	He'll be Dead in Seven days, Voodoo, on February 23, 2004.

Thomas Friedman:	From Beirut to Jerusalem.
Janelle Ramos	E-mail, November 13, 2003.
Steve La Croix Articles	Sure, you can use any of them you want.
Hound Dawg Articles:	Any thing that is not copy righted is fine with me.